"Hidden Souls reaches deep ii
and confronts the darkest lies
receiving the fullness of God's merciful healing grace. Working
through the *Hidden Souls* study has allowed me, and other
survivors of sexual abuse, to embrace the true gift of being God's
precious beloved. This study is essential for the healing journey
of a survivor of sexual abuse."

— Shannon M. Deitz,
Incest and sexual assault survivor,
Founder of Hopeful Hearts Ministry,
Author, Speaker

"Tamara Renee has written a practical and powerful Bible study
that is changing the lives of women who have been devastated
by abuse. *Hidden Souls* draws upon her own life experience and
skillfully weaves profound biblical truth with compelling stories
and practical application. As her pastor, I have seen God use
this study in our own congregation and community in incredible
ways. This will be a useful tool to bring divine healing to
hurting women where you live and minister."

— Dr. Ed Seay,
Senior Pastor of Magnolia's First Baptist Church, Magnolia, Texas

"This study touched my heart like nothing I've ever read. It
reveals, in a very real way, how God can turn tragedy into
triumph. For the first time, the wounds that have shaped my
entire life have begun to heal and my relationship with God is
developing into the one that He and I have so
desperately longed for."

— Pam Stinson,
Pinehurst, Texas

"When Tamara Renee wrote her book from her life experience, it touched me deeply, because I invest in women's lives, through a ministry called Joy Sisters Ladies' Bible Study. It started with seven ladies in my home and has an attendance of 250-300 ladies at this time.

"Through this ladies' Bible study ministry, I met Tamara Renee, who was a young mother and wife looking for answers to many disturbing areas in her life.

"As she discovered scriptural answers to many of her questions and specific needs through Bible study, inspiration began to flow into the writing of her book.

"This book has helped to change many lives of other women who have been traumatized through similar life experiences. I highly recommend this book."

—June Wright,
Magnolia, Texas

"I have seen Tamara apply the principles of biblical truth in her own life and be transformed into a new creation. This study is now working in the lives of others, bringing peace and healing to those who carry scars from abuse."

— Leslie Marie Moursund,
Life Touch Christian Counselor at Magnolia's First Baptist Church, Magnolia, Texas

Hidden Souls

A Bible Study for Women
Seeking Healing from Abuse

TAMARA RENEE

LUCIDBOOKS

Hidden Souls
A Bible Study for Women Seeking Healing from Abuse
Week and Day heading illustrations: Tamara Renee
Headshot photographer: Andi Artze, 2A Photography
Copyright © 2017 by Tamara Renee

Published by Lucid Books in Houston, TX.
www.lucidbookspublishing.com

ISBN-10: 1632961180
ISBN-13: 9781632961181
eISBN-10: 1632961199
eISBN-13: 9781632961198

Special Sales: Most Lucid Books titles are available in special quantity discounts. Custom imprinting or excerpting can also be done to fit special needs. Contact Lucid Books at info@lucidbookspublishing.com.

TABLE OF CONTENTS

Introduction

Liar

If honesty would let me be so bold as to say that word out loud. Harsh as it is, it's been screamed, whispered, battered around in clouds of confusion in my mind. It's ricocheted off the lightning strikes of pain that also scream LIAR! And the storm raged on with no answers as to why someone or something would be so fiendish in the first place. The only thing firmly set inside that storm was the rock-solid conviction that everything was wrong.

At times that word has been a question. When the belief in something was shaken by the reality of something else. With vulnerability chafing as only it can, the question comes out, "Are You a liar?"—softly said, because the strength needed to be angry is just gone for the day. When nothing lines up in the brain as it should, confusion settles in and plays mean little tricks on us—tricks that usually led me to ask the question again and again.

Why, liar, why?!?

This was the word, and the accompanying feeling, that came to my mind when I read things like "The LORD will protect you from all evil" as declared in the Psalms of Holy Truth. Have you ever, like I have a thousand times, said "Really, LORD?" "You will protect me from *all* evil?" Has that question ever been infused with the residual anger gained from a terrible experience—an experience you were most definitely NOT protected from? Have you ever sat there while that experience played over and over in your mind right alongside the seemingly empty promise of protection? Did the anger and disbelief grow inside you with the storm? Did the lightning strikes of fear and pain lure you into believing everyone's a liar? Maybe the road you came down has got you believing that nothing is real and nothing matters and there is absolutely no blasted point to life in general so why even bother...

If that's the case, may I ask you a question?

Why do you still feel? Why do you still get angry? Why do you still ask why?

Okay, that was three questions, but let's get real for a moment. Good gracious, I am well acquainted with all of this. From my earliest memories, my life has been chaos—that's about the best word to describe it. Years and miles of chaos. Experiences that brewed anger and mistrust. Memories that developed nightmares and the unrelenting claws of heartache, so that, even when my body was finally free, my mind wasn't. The "Why?" question has been prompted a time or a thousand. Of course, I went through a period where I didn't believe there was anything greater than me in the universe, because if there were a God, and He promised love but allowed me to be torn apart time and again, then He was the most cruel thing imaginable, and WHY would I want to believe in something like that?

But the truth that kept lingering around in my mind, no matter how hard I tried to kick it out, was that I did believe in something. I was angry, but angry at what? I was hurting, but if nothing mattered, why did I still hurt? I wanted answers! But answers from where??? I saw things in life that mattered. What made them matter? I witnessed beauty and undeniable good. Could I ever be a part of that, and more importantly, why did I still long for connections? Could I ever be anything other than the girl who couldn't relate to anyone? The girl who suffered? The girl on the outside looking in? The stranger?

Then, one day when I was beyond sick of everything in my little world, I had a thought that changed the game. That thought became life to me. It is the basis of this Bible study. The thought was that maybe there was a critical truth resting in those feelings, questions, and anger. There was an attainable silver lining that touched on hope. I realized that I simply could not be angry with something I didn't believe in. Let that soak in for a second: I believed in something.

That was a truth I couldn't shake. And, I am betting, so do you. I just needed to figure out what that "something" was. I had rebelled against the thought of a Creator with a love for His creation for a very long time because my pain ran so deep. But nothing resonated with my mind and my heart the way God did when I truly examined faith. I began to understand that I was still alive so there was still a point. And so are you. There is a point for you.

Let me tell you something else I finally realized. There *is* a liar out there—a grand, cruel liar. But it is not the Lord. I hope this book will help you see evil for what it is and God for who He is. It took me many solid years of fighting to find the truth and be able to one-hundred-percent believe in the words I am typing, but that journey changed my life. I began by flinging that accusation at God, and piece-by-piece, He helped me redirect it to where it belongs. I used to look to God and say "You say You love me? Liar." "You want what's best for me? Liar." "You have good plans for me? (You guessed it:) Liar."

Some of you may be thinking that is a rather bold word to be throwing at God. Who in their right mind has the audacity to speak that way to the Creator of the world? Well…pain does. Pain confuses everything, and it doesn't play nicely with friends, and it doesn't even give a darn about anyone's rules. But maybe you know that, too.

When I hurt, I lashed out. When I hurt, I withdrew. If you try to tell me that, when you hurt, you make cookies and skip in the sunshine, I'm going to call you a liar. The one thing I think I did correctly was to be honest in my pain. When I spoke to God, I brought to the table my questions and my accusations. With every redirection of that word *liar*, God taught me truth. Let me share this with you and see where it takes you. It's got to be better than where you are now—if you are still trying to tread water in a pool that feels more like black, sticky tar.

What do you have to lose?

Week 1

Is He Real? And If So...

Be completely honest with yourself and with God, no matter what that honesty reveals. Remember that you, your small group, and God are the only ones privy to this information. After you complete the week's study, answer these questions again with the truth you have learned from God's Word and the women's testimonies. Compare the two and see if your answers have changed any.

God's Promise: That He will reveal Himself to you. That He wants a personal relationship with you.

Do you believe this? _____

Why? Why not? _____

_____

_____

Satan's Lie: God is not real. God is not the only God. God is not powerful. God will not talk to you.

Do you believe this? _____

Why? Why not? _____

_____

_____

Plans? What Plans?

When terrible things happen to people, especially at very young ages, or via people who were supposed to protect them and not harm them, it is natural to have doubts about God. So very many things are just wrong in your life that it is hard to believe God would allow these things to happen to someone He claims to love. Pain confuses truth, but the Truth never changes. The first thing you have to ask yourself is: Is God real? Many people in this world will try to convince you that He is not real. People live passing lives on this earth. Their ideas, philosophies, desires, educational techniques, and just about everything else change with the generations. Constant evolution. Constant change. But the Word of God does not change. I have seen God speak to people clearly through His Word. I have doubted it, having come from a long history of serious childhood abuse myself. I have sought to prove it wrong. The funny thing is that the more I tried to find fault in the Bible, the more I studied it, the more God used it to heal me. If someone had told the girl I was at fourteen that I would ever feel whole and happy, I would have scoffed at them. But God had different plans for me. He also has different plans for you.

In Psalm 34:8, David challenges the people to "Taste and see that the LORD is good." Will you? Will you look past any ideas you may have formed from your pain or anger? God needs only a willingness from His people to seek out the truth, and He will reveal Himself to them. If we could heal ourselves, we would not need a Savior. If we knew all the answers, we would not need to pray to the Creator. If we think we have it all together, then we need Him more than anyone!

You may be familiar with this verse, as it is commonly used, but look it up anyway and jot down what it says. Jeremiah 29:11:

_____

_____

_____

_____

God knows the plans He has for you. Plans that may sound very different from the plans people have had for you. Oh yes, people had terrible plans for you, and they were allowed their free will, just as you are—God did not create puppets. Real love and real relationships only come from free choice. But God knew what some people would do with this great gift He gave to them. He knew people would use and abuse free choice. The world is full of selfishness and deceit, so God provided a way for all to obtain healing from others' choices—even from our own choices. That is where the second part of this Scripture comes into play. This part of the Scripture is not usually read, but it is by far the most important. The simple fact is that God has plans for everyone, but it is up to us to find out what those plans are. Some of us will, and some of us will just keep stumbling around in the dark, trying to make sense of this world on our own.

Read and write out Jeremiah 29:12, 13: _____

_____

_____

_____

When you seek God with ALL your heart, He is there waiting to be found by you. Do not think that God is blind to the life you have lived. Do not let someone fool you into believing that He does not care or that He is not real. It is like when Ahaz was king of Judah (Isa. 7:10). God told Ahaz to ask Him for a sign to help him stand firm in his faith. Verse 11 says, "Ask the LORD your God for a sign, whether in the deepest depths or in the highest heights." God knows we must have some strengthening of our faith if we are going to be able to walk with Him. It is my prayer for you that you will open your heart and receive these signs, so that your faith and healing will be strong.

The communication lines are opened through prayer alone, as stated in verse 12 of Jeremiah 29. Prayer is any time you say, "Lord, can we have a little chat?" It is impossible to have a relationship with someone who will not talk to you. It is even more impossible to help someone who will not talk to you. You may feel funny speaking to something you cannot see. You may not know how to hear when God speaks back. Here are a few easy steps to follow that will hopefully help in this area:

1. Remember what Matthew 6:5-8 says. Get alone with God so you can be completely focused, open, and honest. He knows what's in your heart, anyway. He also knows what you need before you even ask.

2. Here's the hard part (especially if you are a girl like me). After you have prayed, you have to be...quiet. Psalm 37:7: "Be still before the LORD and wait patiently for Him." Psalm 46:10: "Be still, and know that I am God."

We are starting a journey that will, at times, be very ugly for you. I am so proud of you that you are here, trying to move on, trying to find answers to questions that may have held you bound to the past for a very long time. Please do not give up. With diligence, you *will* make it through. It is time to move on. Let's do this together, and we will know joy in the end. Don't let any more be taken from you. Your wounds will be healed, and your mistakes will be cleansed. Be brave, my sister.

Close today by asking God to bring to mind a time that you think He may have been showing Himself to you. If you can recall no such time, think of a testimony someone else has shared with you. Sometimes it really helps to write it down so we can pull strength from it later.

_____

_____

_____

_____

_____

_____

_____

_____

_____

_____

_____

_____

_____

_____

_____

_____

_____

_____

_____

Why Does He Let These Things Happen?

Go ahead and get it out. Ask Him WHY. (Grab some tissues and, if need be, some things to throw that you don't mind breaking.) Why did You let _____ do _____? Cut any pretense and ask God for all those answers you never got from man. But brace yourself, because if you seek Him in honesty, He WILL answer you. God knows you need answers in order to move on. He is just waiting for your heart to be ready to hear them. If you still spill out an automatic answer of "I'm fine," then I would wager you may not be ready. These are ugly questions, and as long as they are kept in secrecy and darkness, they will continue to keep you in turmoil. But when something is brought into the light, whether we completely understand it or not, Satan's power to use it against us is removed. We begin to breathe air that is a little less thick, and somehow it truly does get easier to admit that we may not be "fine" sometimes.

So, let us begin with: **Why does God let these things happen?**

When I became a new believer and began to trudge through the ugliness of what life used to be, I had to understand why God would allow these awful things to happen. In a way, I simply could not follow God without some kind of sense being made out of the way people are allowed to hurt each other. Or why children are born with severe medical issues. Or why people die such awful deaths. I mean, the list can go on and on.

Let's tackle the easier of these highways first. Go with me to John 9. I believe, out of all those who walked with Jesus, John understood His love the most. The more a person can understand God's love, the easier it is to see the truth in any given situation.

Read John 9:1-11.

Herein lies the answer to a very common question. Is someone being punished for a sin they committed? Are babies born with ailments to punish the sins of their parents? The disciples thought so. But write out what Jesus teaches them in verse 3. _____

_____

_____

Jesus clears this up pretty nicely and then displays the manifestation of His truth. He heals the blind man and sends him home to testify.

There is one more thing to consider here: Do not assume that the blind man had not been under God's merciful care all his life. There were most definitely struggles that came with being blind. He must have had fears and been lonely. Darkness had the possibility of taking on a whole new meaning if the man had been without the Maker. But he was not; no, he most certainly was not. Have you ever known a person who suffered more than their fair share, yet still had sweetness in them? What do you think preserves those qualities if not God? _____

_____

Now read what Jesus says in Matthew 11:28-30. Rest for your souls through ANY burden is what God offers. God doesn't callously leave the afflicted martyred on the earth for His glory alone. He is with them every step of the way, whether they know it or not. He tells us this over and over in the Psalms. Psalm 18:28, Psalm 27:10, Psalm 34:18, Psalm 139:12. There are many, many more. Check them out when you have a minute. Let them warm you.

Now let's take a look at when children are caught up in man's plans. For some reason, I was really stuck on the whole Sodom and Gomorrah story in Genesis 19. Children must have lived there. Why did they have to die? Since God declared the cities completely wicked and unrighteous, He destroyed them. Ouch. (Understatement). Oftentimes, God's power and authority are displayed in great severity in the Old Testament to show the people that He was not to be taken lightly. But were these children wicked? (Was I wicked as a child? The mind can put two completely unrelated things together when the truth is absent.) Then, I read the account in Isaiah 7:14-16. Go with me here and read again verses 15-16. This passage gave me hope that children who are not old enough to understand right and wrong are totally covered by God's grace. The children who perished as a result of man's sin in these cities were taken home to be with the LORD. God did this to save them before men had a chance to corrupt them so fully that they would never know their God. Man's capacity for wickedness is appalling. God chose to intervene in this case. He chose not to let the sins continue in Sodom and Gomorrah because they affected *every* man, woman, and child, and it was never going to stop. God's choice of when, and when not to, intervene is sometimes very painful and hard for us to understand. I pray this mystery will reveal itself to us throughout this study.

Christ also treated children with the utmost tenderness. He says in Mark 9:37 that whoever is kind to a child is kind to Him. He rebukes the disciples in Mark 10:13-16 when they try to keep children away from His blessing. In Luke 17:1-3, Jesus makes it clear that it would be better for a man to be thrown into the sea than to cause a little one to sin. Maybe the answer I was looking for with these questions was that, *Yes*, God loved me when I was a child. Do you think God loved you when you were small? Or when you were helpless? Do you think God loves you now? _____

_____

_____

_____

It may not have felt like anyone loved you or even really saw you, but they did. Women (and men) of all ages suffer different levels of abuse that range from one inappropriate, uncomfortable act to multiple horrendous, life-shattering acts. The resulting confusion and pain are the same. No matter the level of abuse, please understand that no amount of pain is ever insignificant. I can't tell you how many times I have heard someone try to downplay their suffering because they knew about my life and they thought I had had it worse. I may have had it worse, or I may not have, but that is not the point. The point is: pain is pain and, mercifully, God applies the same love to all.

Why did God let these things happen? The answer begins with God's greatest gifts to man: free will and free choice. When God created man, He wanted to have an open, loving relationship with us. Can you love someone you are forced to love? Can you be friends with someone who forces you to do anything—totally controlled by someone else's desires, with no will of your own? No, we cannot. The power of love is in *choice*. God also *chose* to love us, no matter what—no matter what it costs us, and no matter what it costs Him.

Sin entered the world when Satan played dirty pool with Eve and she *chose* to do something God told her not to do (Gen. 3). Something here to take note of is that *before* there was sin, there was *choice*. That is why Jesus knocks on a door and does not barrel through. A Mighty God is the God of Israel, as Jacob christened God after he wrestled with Him all evening long in Genesis 32. God has the power, and the right, to force every living thing to be sweet and compliant and wonderful to each other. He can make us all love Him and each other. But He would not be a loving God if He did so. Therefore, people are allowed to make their own choices and, therefore, sometimes people get hurt. Sometimes people get terribly hurt.

Read Revelation 3:19-22.

Fill in these blanks: "Here I am! I _____ at the door and _____. If anyone _____ my _____ and _____ the door, I will _____ and eat with that person, and they with me. To him who is_____, I will give the right to sit with me..."

He will not force His truth into your life, but He stands waiting for you to claim it. This study will help you if you will work through the darkness with me. I have been many places you have been. I have many scars from people who chose to harm me, reminding me of the evil in this world. But I have seen God's healing work in my life and in others' lives. I have seen women laugh so beautifully from the inside out, where they used to be only full of sorrow. God needs only a willing heart to create a miracle. We must simply open the door. Open the door, please.

Conclude today by making a commitment to God, and to yourself, to diligently follow through with opening the door. Jot down some things that you think may attempt to keep you from reaching this goal. Maybe it is fear of someone finding out, maybe it is that your time is very limited, maybe you don't quite believe that the Bible is God's truth for all mankind, maybe you are afraid you will remember things you think are better left forgotten. Whatever the case may be, ask God to help you. He will.

_____

_____

_____

_____

_____

_____

_____

_____

_____

_____

_____

_____

_____

_____

_____

_____

Where Was He When...?

I am so glad to see you have decided to continue. Today, the power of testimony will be used to try and help you understand where God was when you were being abused. It is hard to think that God is everywhere, at all times, seeing everything that goes on in this world. It is even harder, when you have suffered, to think that God knew everything that would ever happen to you and allowed it anyway. One woman I know had been raped repeatedly by her father when she was only in her eleventh year of life. Boy, did she have some questions for God. And some anger. But after many years of defeat, she opened her heart and mind to learn God's truth. Now, she is willing to share what He told her, because it changed her life.

Before I share with you her story, look up Revelation 12:1-12. Read the whole twelve verses and then fill in these blanks (I know it's a long one, but it's an important one!):

"They _____ him (Satan) by the blood of _____ _____ (Christ) and by the word of their _____" (v. 11 KJV).

The way to fight back is first to accept the blood of the Lamb; let it wash over you. Accept that His death on the cross defeated any power that Satan claimed. Accept that Jesus did not have to suffer in that way, but He did, so that we could know Him and draw strength from Him—and then go tell what He has done! In a world full of people who have to see to believe, our testimonies provide them with glasses. Sometimes it will be scary and very difficult to speak a testimony. We are not always called to do this. Sometimes we are just called to be someone's friend or simply proof that life after tragedy is possible. But sometimes, like my friend here, we are called to tell people who have suffered along the same lines as we have suffered what God has done in our lives. We do this so that people can see that God is real. That God is good. We do this to give them strength. We do this to take Satan's power away from him. The way to fight back is to fight with the knowledge that the ultimate battle is already won. Now, at this point in your life, Satan can only take what you will give him. I can't think of a better reason to be brave.

The following testimony holds a critical aspect of God's truth. I will allow our sister the use of my pen now...

Pain has a way of capturing all the soul's focus. Pain creates a fog that, with a little heat, can hide all the good and grace we have in our lives. I had been brokenhearted and lonely from the earliest point of my memory. Then learning, and believing, that God was there, watching over every minute of my life, made me angry. I felt cheated. It was all just so...wrong. Why, Lord! Why did you let them do these things to me, a helpless child? An innocent, at the time. They tormented me and then they laughed about it. They took my childhood and parts of my future. They took my security and my laughter. They left scars upon my skin and then criticized the very scars they inflicted. They snuffed out any flame of trust within the little person I was. I could not even get away from them in my dreams.

One day my temper flared and I yelled out to this "Loving God" I was learning about at church. I said, "WHY did You let them take EVERYTHING from me! You knew what was going to happen, so WHERE WERE YOU!?"

Pause for one moment here. God did answer me that day, calmly and quietly. He is big enough to handle our truth. He is not going to strike you with lightning for being real in all your emotions, questions, and doubts. This raw place is where, when He does answer us, it can change our lives. The answer He gave me was the moment I began to melt away some of the selfish nature our world foments. This was the root of true forgiveness, for myself for the things I had done wrong, and from me to those who had harmed me.

God said to me that day within the raging of my heart: "I was surrounding your love. I would not allow anyone to take that away from you, or from Me."

In those simple words, God struck me silent. God's truth washed through me like that river we sometimes sing of going to. He quieted me with His love. He explained to me how He saved my ability to love and enjoy things in my life. He made it clear to me that He did not save my love for me alone, but for Him as well. He was not willing to allow me to be lost to Him forever because of the things people would do to me.

Where was God when you were being abused? He was firmly wrapped around your ability to love. He was protecting the only part of you that could possibly find its way back to Him through the hell you lived. It's not the head, but the heart, that leads us home when your heart is led by Christ. God makes a way for ALL hearts to return to him. Yes, He saw you in that terrible state. He saw them hurting you as He allowed the world to keep turning. Please do not think that He sat by idly, unmoved and unaffected, while you suffered. Every single tear that poured from your eye was kept by your Father in heaven.

Read these words and know where your tears went when you thought they fell deafly into the abyss: "Record my misery; list my tears on your scroll—are they not in Your record?" —Psalm 56:8.

Now read how important each and every teardrop is to God. Not as a collective whole, but singularly, individually, God will wipe the eye of every soul who has ever shed pain upon their cheek when we meet Him face-to-face (Rev. 21:4). It is not only that there will be no more suffering when we stand face-to-face with the LORD; it is that He will show us how He cares by acknowledging that suffering and soothing it with His touch.

Read in Revelation 21:3-8 how He will display His love for you when He finally says, "Enough is enough." What does verse 7 say?

_____

_____

Write out Proverbs 4:23 (from the pen of Solomon—a man who desired wisdom above all else). God told him what was to be protected first.

"Above _____ else guard your _____, for it is the well spring of _____."

When you were not capable of guarding your heart, God did it for you. He still does this for us today, and He will continue to do this until we return to Him in death, because we are HIS children. We can make choices on our own that can come from a heart that has been led astray. Proverbs 12:20 speaks of deceit filling hearts that plot evil. But then, Psalm 51:10 speaks of cleansing. Write out the prayer of a man who knew what it meant to allow his heart to be led astray: _____

_____

_____

David made so many mistakes in his lifetime. Many of them had terrible repercussions, but he *always* turned back to God with a plea for forgiveness, mercy, and cleansing. David fully understood there was nothing God's love couldn't cover.

Conclude today by making a list of the people and the things that you love, past or present. Record things you enjoy, like tasty foods, favorite colors, funny stories, an outfit that you really love. What kind of things do you enjoy doing—movies, books, sports, music, skydiving, painting, rock collecting, other hobbies? What smells make you stop and breathe deeply? Freshly baked cookies, cut grass, rain, buttered popcorn, someone's home? Think of everything that brings a smile to you. Think of what your life would be like if God had allowed Satan to take even the joy of these things from you. From tallest to smallest, write down as many as you can think of.

_____

_____

_____

His Ways Are Higher

What does home feel like to you? _____

_____

_____

Have you ever felt like you had a home? Where? _____

_____

_____

Or, like many women who have been abused, have you felt like a stranger during times in your life, no matter where you were? When? _____

_____

_____

We have got to focus a bit on this point, because we just don't live forever. When we die, we are going somewhere. Either you go home, or you finally realize that there was more to life than you would have believed, and at that terrible moment, you are not allowed entry. God gives you a lifetime to choose what will be enforced in a single breath.

Most people who have been abused have had to live in secret, hiding, sometimes moving from place to place. Sometimes they have been shuffled around like a piece of furniture no one could seem to fit into their home. They were never really looked at. They were not particularly looked for. It seemed to be better for other people if they just took their problems elsewhere. Well, there is one little problem with this when you are a child. Children need looking after and to be cared for. And there is one huge problem with this when those children come of age and are put out into a fast-paced, self-centered world. Where is a stranger to go? Where can they find a home where they have comfort, security and the ability to be themselves?

Hold that thought for a moment while we work something out.

Do you believe that the Bible was inspired by God, written through man? Why or why not? _____

_____

_____

For those of you who are not sold on this idea, I understand. The only thing I can tell you is that I once had the same kind of questions—so I went in search of answers. I began to study what the Bible taught. My prayer for you is that you will do the same, and through that process you will come closer to your God.

Look up 2 Timothy 3:16, 17 and summarize the verses here:

_____

_____

_____

Now read: Isaiah 55:9-11:

> "As the heavens are higher than the earth,
> so are My ways higher than your ways
> and My thoughts than your thoughts.
> As the rain and the snow come down from heaven,
> and do not return to it without watering the earth
> and making it bud and flourish,
> so that it yields seed for the sower and bread for the eater,
> so is My word that goes out from My mouth:
> It will not return to Me empty,
> But will accomplish what I desire
> and achieve the purpose for which I sent it."

For what purpose do you think God sends out His Word? ____

_____

_____

In case you were not sure how to answer this, fill in the blanks of the very next part of this Scripture. _____ will go out in _____ and be led forth in _____. (v. 12a)

YOU! God's word is for you. The word is not only for you to better know your creator, but for Him to be able to lead you through your life in *peace and joy*. These may be foreign concepts to you, my dear sister. They sure were to me. As much as I longed for peace in my head and under my skin, I did not believe it was possible. But that was because I had not yet met my Savior.

Let's go back to this concept of home. I knew only one person in my early life who could comfort me with her mere presence. She was someone else's Granny, but she loved me anyway. She was a tough ol' broad, born in the days of hard work and no complaining. When she cooked, everyone came over. When she cussed, everyone got out of the way. And when you just did not think you could take it any longer, you could rest your tired head on her shoulder, and for a moment, her love made it all okay. She was like this for everyone who knew her. She was the closest place I ever felt to home. It broke my heart when she passed on. I would never find another like Mrs. Thelma Morrow. Have you ever known someone like this?

_____

I think Jesus must have had this same quality. He must have just felt right for people to have flocked to Him the way they did. He was humble and gentle and loving and kind. He had all those fruits of the Spirit we learn about in Galatians 5 nailed down. "I led them with cords of human kindness, with ties of love. To them I was like one who lifts a little child to the cheek, and I bent down to feed them" (Hos. 11:4). There was no pretense or ulterior motive in His goodness. He loved people like Mrs. Morrow loved me, just because He wanted to.

Just as we do not always understand God's plans now, people did not really understand Jesus back then. He was, shockingly, not the great warrior king Israel had been looking for when they thought of a Messiah. His teaching was sometimes too simple for people to understand. Jesus taught in black and white.

> Either you followed God, or you followed something else. Look up Matthew 6:24.
> Either you forgave, or you were not forgiven. Look up Matthew 6:15.
> Either you accepted the peace He offered, or you didn't. Look up Luke 19:42.
> Either you went home when your life ended on earth, or you were separated from God for eternity. Write out John 3:16, even if you have read it a thousand times: _____

_____

We have a home in heaven. While we are here on earth, we are granted a precious taste of what living there will feel like when we come into God's presence. When we connect with a truth from God's Word, we see it. Or when a Scripture touches our heart in a way that nothing else can, we feel that warmth and peace. You may never have known a place on earth that felt like home to you. You may have been harmed greatly by the people who lived in your home. You may not understand what it is like to feel like all is right in the world because you are at home, or because so-and-so is with you. I understand how lonely and unsettling that can be. I did not have a safe home until one was created for my children.

But God did not create you to be homeless. Use the tools He gave you to find it. This study can be one of those tools, if you will allow God to use it in your life.

Conclude today's study by asking God to bring to mind a Scripture that has become rather special to you. Why has it touched your heart so? If you do not have one yet, look back over the week's lessons and see if there is a Scripture that made sense to you in some way. Write it here.

_____

_____

Why Was I Made?

There are different types of love that God created to enrich our lives. Today, we will explore these types of love in the pure form in which they were intended to be given and received. One very ugly aspect of sexual abuse is how these "loves" can be used to hurt us, control us, or confuse us. This is NOT what God intended. Today's lesson will be difficult for many, but hang in there. You are not alone. You are going to need a tad bit more time for today's lesson.

Crack your knuckles and open your Bible. We are going to fight lies with truth. Where someone told you that they loved you while they were hurting you, we will see in Scripture how very wrong they were. Where someone lied to you about what love is, we will learn what love is not. We were created for God's delight, not for man's sickness. God put us on this earth for a reason. He does not want us to simply breathe in and out each day, labor, eat, sleep, and then die. How mundane a life would that be? He created us to have relationships with each other. He created us to love! He wants our lives to be filled with joy. You may not yet think this is possible, and please hear my heart when I tell you that there was a time I sat on that island with you. Look up Ecclesiastes 5:20 and tell me what it says:

_____

_____

_____

I normally use the NIV translation, but here I really like how the NLT puts it: "They take no time to brood over the past." Let's stop for a second and ask God to bring us to this place, where the joy in our hearts eclipses the ugliness of the past. It will take some time, but that time will come. Pray also for discernment as we go through this day on love. Understanding the pure forms of love is critical to healing. We cannot move on without this knowledge. If you'd like, write your prayer out here:

_____

_____

_____

_____

_____

_____

_____

In the Word, there are three types of love taught to us. They are *eros*, *philos*, and *agape*. Let's break these down to get a better understanding of what they are and why they are indeed different.

EROS: Grasping Love. Literally, a longing and desire. This is where physical temptation comes from. Man has perverted this type of love by giving into lust with abandon. Our culture today says nearly anything is permissible. The selfishness of man says take, take, take. The sickness of Satan says there are no limits to desire. When these two things are effectively mixed, the concoction is frightening. It is the Evil One alone who says a man or woman can lust after or exploit a child of any age. It is the goal of Satan to get man to believe that physical intimacy means nothing more than a sexual act. Sexual intimacy in any form, from sight to intercourse, was never meant to be casual or harmful. This type of love is probably the most confused in your mind. Jot down ANY questions you have in this area to be discussed in your small group. Do not be embarrassed. Pure, natural desire is not wrong—Satan has just taken something beautiful and completely distorted it.

In order to see this love in a pure context, we need the black-and-white of Scripture. Go to Genesis 24. Read the account of Issac and Rebekah in verses 50-67. Verses 1-49 recount Abraham's servant setting out to look for a wife for Issac. After travel and prayer the servant encounters a kind young woman.

What does verse 57 say about Rebekah's right to choose? _____

_____

What does verse 67 say Issac did before he touched her? _____

_____

Also in verse 67, what does it say happened after they were married? _____

The NIV reads: "and he loved her." The KJV reads: "and he took her." Here *loved* and *took* go hand-in-hand. Rebekah agreed, they married, Issac loved purely from his heart. This is how physical intimacy was designed by God to be between man and woman.

There is one more extremely important thing to consider. Go to Song of Songs 2:7 (some translations title this book "Song of Solomon," after the writer). We will dig into this deeper later, but take special note of this verse. "Do not arouse or awaken my love until she pleases" (NASB). Your sexuality was and still is precious. It was to be left alone to ripen and develop naturally. If this innocence is taken from you too soon, it will have lasting effects on your body and mind. But take heart, there is healing and restoration.

PHILOS: Friend love. The love one has toward a friend or companion. Again, write ANY questions you may have down and bring them to group.

Many women who come from sexual abuse do not know if it is possible to be "just friends" with a man. For some reason, the abuse planted a seed in their mind that connects most men with the woman's sexuality. Sometimes these women do not even realize they are turning up the sexuality when men are present, but it often happens. This is a side effect of the abuse. A conditioning, so to speak, creating a confusion of who you are and what you were made for. This is where a boundary was not learned. This is not initially the woman's fault, but it does need to be discussed, so that, if this chain is present, it can be broken. Maybe our deep craving for connection is so strong that we revert to an action that encourages some form of connection. Maybe we think that this is all a man *really* wants out of a woman. This is false. It is possible to separate sexuality and friendship. Your worth does not come from whether someone desires you in that way or not. All men do NOT only see a woman in a sexual way.

Let's look at one reason God gives us friendship love. Turn to Luke 15:8, 9. This woman was stressing out when she lost her coin. When she found it, she called her girlfriends and they all rejoiced together. If she had not found it, someone would have come to help her look for it. This is a great example of philos love. We are granted the ability to love a friend so that they may walk with us, and we with them, through life. Open your heart to your friends. Do not be kept in solitude because someone, somewhere down the line, could betray you. That is a real possibility, but there are far more possibilities for God-honoring, joyous friendships. Make a little time for them. Friends are gifts to our lives, and we can be great gifts to others.

Who are some of your closest girlfriends? _____

_____

Do you know any men that you consider friends? _____

_____

AGAPE: Caring love. This type of love is less a feeling and more a response based on a need. This love is sacrificial and demonstrative. Examples of this would be doing things like stopping what you were doing to listen to someone, or going out of your way to help someone with no personal gain, or being happy for someone anyway if they obtained something that you really wanted. God displays this love throughout His entire Word. The greatest display of God's agape love to us was, and will forever be, the sacrificial death of His son.

The meaning of agape is beautifully broken down in 1 Corinthians 13:4-8. Read these verses.

The first fruit of the Spirit is agape love. All the other fruits—joy, peace, patience, kindness, goodness, faithfulness, gentleness, and self-control—are not possible without love at the engine of that train.

> Love (agape) (definitions taken from *The Complete Word Study Dictionary: New Testament*, and *Strong's Exhaustive Concordance of The Bible*):

is patient—someone who is able to avenge himself, yet refrains from doing so

is kind—generally means to show oneself useful

does not envy—"to be zealous"; connotes a passionate sense of jealousy

does not boast—brag

is not proud—read Proverbs 13:10 and write out one of the many things pride brings: _____

is not rude—to behave in an ugly, indecent, unseemly, or unbecoming manner

is not self-seeking—read 2 Timothy 3:2 and jot down the only thing self-seeking people can love: _____

is not easily angered—remember that anger is an emotion that comes from God. The problem lies in what is done with the anger.

does not delight in evil—read 1 Peter 5:8. Who delights in evil?

rejoices with the truth—read John 14:6. What is Truth?

always protects—"to cover over in silence"—meaning to not express the faults of others

always trusts—having faith in someone

always hopes—to expect with desire

always perseveres—"to remain under," or—as we would understand it—"to hang in there"

never fails—love like this, applied to and accepted by ANY life, completely changes the person

Okay, that is a lot to soak in. If you come from any place I have lived, you may never have been shown this love. So often we can feel like failures for not being able to be or do these things. You may not even be able to understand this love yet. At times, we can be caring and patient. At times, we can be kind and forgiving. But no matter how hard we try, we are not capable of fully, continually, without ever failing, expressing this love to everyone we know. However, we *can* express it more as we draw closer to God's presence, because God is the origin and the only true source of agape.

God chooses to pour His love through us, when we seek Him, so that we may be able to love others. This is one way in which God is shown to the world. He does this so that when you want to give up on someone or something, you don't. So that when you want to yell at someone, you don't. So that when you get angry at someone, you can be calmed, even though you would much rather kick them instead. This love is not possible without God. If it were, we would not need Him. If we did not need Him, we would not know Him.

He also pours this love through us so that we may know and be able to feel what it is to be loved. Someone may have told you that if you loved them, you would do _____ for them. Many abusers (sexual, physical, and mental) use this tactic to get what they want. This is a demonstration of control and manipulation. Love was not meant to be used in this way. These people do not understand love.

Read 1 Corinthians 13:2. What do you have if you do not have love? Look back to day three if you need a reminder of what ability God saved inside you when someone tried to take everything good from you: **the ability to:** _____

Did you learn anything new about the definition of love today? Can you remember a time when love was misused and manipulated by abusers in your life? _____

_____

_____

_____

_____

_____

Week 2

Sometimes You Have to Go Back

God's Promise: The truth will set you free. John 8:32

Do you believe this? _____

Why? Why not? _____

_____

_____

Satan's Lie: You made it up. It's ALL your fault.

Do you believe this? _____

Why? Why not? _____

_____

_____

Look Straight at It . . .

Last week during group, you had the opportunity to get your past history of abuse out in the open. Some of you may still be stuck in a situation where you are currently being abused. It is a very sad fact that many parents are mentally abusive to grown children in an attempt to control their lives. It is also an unfortunate reality that many spouses are physically and sexually abusive to their partners. If your husband physically forces you to have sex with him, that is still abuse. You need to get help. If your husband physically harms you, and you fear his temper and anger, that is abuse. Please be brave and speak up. Seek biblical advice from your pastor or a counselor. You may feel like you have no other options, and that is exactly how an abusive person wants to keep things. They want you to be confused and feel like everything is your fault, so they can control you. But there is help for you, if you seek it. You do not deserve abuse.

We are going to focus on the very difficult task of looking at our pasts today. You may have shared everything in group, or maybe not. It may be ugly, awful, terrifying, or nicely tucked under a pretty sofa, but you have to look straight at it in order to deal with it. We are not here to relive the past. We are here to break away from the past. In order to do that, we must not run from it.

One teenager shared this with me:

I had to get away. I stole a car and drove it until I couldn't drive it anymore. Then I hitchhiked until I reached the shoreline of the last state on the highway. Had there been a path through the ocean I would have taken it. I just couldn't deal with things any longer. It's in the moving, I think that does it. I am getting away. I am in motion. I am not being held down. It seemed perfect logic at the time. But then, eventually, I still had to come back. Surprise, Surprise, the problems were there, right where I left them.

No matter what we do today, it will not change what happened yesterday. But you are more than what happened to you. Yesterday does not have the power to write your tomorrows unless you allow it pen and paper. You are a person with a future that is defined by God's love for you.

Read Acts 13:6-12.

Who was Elymas? (v. 8) _____

What was he attempting to do to the proconsul who had requested to hear the word of God from Barnabas and Saul? (v. 8)

_____

Any time you begin to seek God in earnest, Satan will not be pleased. His people will do everything they can in order to turn you away from the Lord. Saul calls them deceitful enemies of everything that is right. There is only one way to combat this.

Write out what Saul did in verse 9: _____

_____

Saul looked straight at Elymas and rebuked him powerfully. How was Saul able to do this?

Check one: ___ He had become a powerful Christian on his own.

    ___ Barnabas helped him.

    ___ He was filled with the Holy Spirit

    ___ Elymas had given up.

By the power of the Holy Spirit within Saul, he was able to duel with a child of the devil and win. On his own, he would not have succeeded. That is why God never leaves us on our own.

Read John 14:15-17.

What does Jesus call the Holy Spirit? A _____

and the _____

How long will the Holy Spirit be with us? _____

Let's take a look at the other side of this story now. Saul calls Elymas a child of the devil. Since there are so many different scenarios in which abuse occurs, we need to bring clarity into our study. An enemy taken lightly is the most dangerous enemy of all. We must never underestimate the ability of Satan to manipulate and distort anything he comes into contact with. We are focusing here on sexual abuse. Some of these crimes were committed by obviously evil people, but some of the perpetrators were very cunning in their ability to mask who they really were. Some of you have been raped, many at very young ages. That is clearly outside of God's will and was not done by someone in relationship with Him. Some of you were molested, maybe once, maybe repeatedly, and forced to do things that should never have happened. The same evil can be blamed for the person who did this to you. These acts were being carried out by someone clearly not serving God. If the person who hurt you was not serving God and they committed these crimes, then they were serving another.

Read John 8:42-47. Here, Jesus tells us about the father of lies. We see a little of his nature and how others follow him in this passage: "He was a _____ from the _____, not holding to the _____, for there is _____ truth in him" (v. 44). As far as those people who harmed you go, at some point in their lives, Satan lied to them also. And they followed him.

Read about the characteristics of false teachers and their destruction in 2 Peter 2:14, 15, 18, 19.

I hope that the characteristics of these people stood out in bold relief to you. I pray you will make the connection that true servants of God do not follow in the way of these false teachers. Look closely at the person described here. Bold, unashamed of their wrongs, arrogant, slanderers, liars, even if they display moments of feeling guilty for their actions. Read again verse 14. How do these people live? "With eyes full of _____, they never stop _____; they _____ the _____; they are in _____—an accursed brood!" Do not miss the point here that they are very good at what they do. Their hearts are black as night, while their outward appearance can blend into any setting—chameleons of the worst sort. It is from here that wickedness is taught to the people who abused you. Satan is due a certain amount of respect, not for his glory by any means, but for us to be aware of who, and how powerful, our enemy is. You cannot run from him. He will follow. Eventually you must fight, or you will fall.

We are well acquainted with this aspect of the world we live in. But do not allow Satan the victory of getting you to believe this is all there is in our world. Draw comfort from every bit of goodness you see around you. Know that God deals with them accordingly. Read 2 Peter 2:4, 5, 9 and see for yourself.

Bring this ugliness into the light and let God wash through it. You may be afraid of bringing up things you don't remember clearly, or even at all. Trust that God will only bring to mind what you are able to deal with now. As you get stronger and more secure in His truth, you can deal with other things, if need be. Or, people may have told you things that you are not sure really happened. Pray for truth and clarity; its light will come.

First John 1:5 declares: "God is light; in Him there is no darkness."

Psalm 18:28 tells us that God can turn ANY darkness into light. There are some depths that ONLY God can illuminate.

Was there anything, that for whatever reason, you could not tell in your small group about your abuse? Do you believe that God is powerful enough to cut through ANY darkness from your past? Take a moment to ask God to help you uncover anything that has the potential to harm. This is why you are here working through this study.

_____

_____

DAY 2

Issues: Anger

Now that we have spent some time going over some less-than-pretty things in our lives, it may be easier to see where some of our issues come from. We are here because we are in search of healing. That means we have to look at the whole enchilada. We can focus only on what has been done to us, but I'll tell you this: you won't still be here for dessert. That delicious pudding-filled chocolate cake, or whatever suits your fancy, is worth a little heartburn.

Anger, fear, bitterness, lack of trust—the list can really go on and on. We will talk about anger today, and look at more of them later. If you are reading this right now, there is a very good chance anger has been a coat you have worn in every color.

How would you like to respond when someone lets you down, makes you mad, or treats you unfairly? _____

_____

_____

In actuality, how do you respond? _____

_____

_____

Where do you think your anger comes from—the root of your flash point? No, this is not a loaded question. Spell it out. Don't leave anything out. _____

_____

What do you think the purpose of anger is? _____

_____

_____

Millions of dollars are made each year by self-help authors and psychiatrists attempting to teach people how to deal with their anger. Anger can tear a person apart. It can push loved ones away. It can become a monster forcing the creation of little eggshell-walking, tiptoeing people wherever it goes. Anger is equally as destructive on the health of its victims as it is on their relationships. I was angry for a long time. Sometimes I could take off my coat and sometimes I couldn't. Even after healing began and the anger started to die down, I still did not understand the beast. Then I read a few things while studying to write this material that made perfect sense to me.

First: Continual anger is twofold. Component one: the demand of an unfulfilled need, coupled with component two: a reaction of punishment.

Second: Anger is an emotion that comes from God.

Going back to the first point, it is understandable that anger can come from an unmet need. "So-and-so did not protect me and I got hurt; it made me angry. Now I am going to punish them by staying mad." "Hubby is not treating me right when he doesn't call if he is going to be late, so I am going to give the dog his dinner and go to bed without talking to him. Take that, Hubby." Hubby may be taking that for a week or so. Really, these scenarios are endless (I have a good one where I threw a homemade peach cobbler out a window while hubby stood with his fork in hand and a very comical expression on his face).

Can you remember a recent event like this in your life where you may have acted in continual anger? _____

_____

Have you recognized any deep-seated anger at the person who abused you, or at other people indirectly involved? _____

_____

It is natural to be angry with them. I would be a little concerned for you if you were not. Anger IS an emotion from God that lets you know that something is wrong. What you do with that anger is a gift of your free will. If someone physically slaps you in the face, chances are you are going to be very angry. This is a natural reaction. Look at one instance when God got very angry with His people of Judah. They were treating God very poorly, and He responded in anger.

Read Lamentations 3:43, 44.

Now look at something very interesting in these verses. Verse 43 states that God covered Himself with anger. That word "covered" is *cakak*, which, literally translated from Hebrew, means "entwine as a screen, fence in, cover over, protect, or defend." This word means a different thing than the typical word meaning "a garment or clothing" or "to clothe." This "covered" literally means God was protecting and defending Himself from the people's continual sins. Then, He disciplined them. Remember that God disciplines those He loves. It is the only way we grow when we have our hardheaded, selfish hats on. Then, again, in verse 44, it states that God "covered" Himself with a cloud, and no prayers could get through to Him.

I don't know about you, but these verses chill me to the bone. God loves us, there is no doubt about that. Once His, nothing can ever separate us from Him. However, our continual sin can cause God to cover Himself so that our discipline is necessary. He will *choose not to hear our prayers.* When we are that angry at somebody, we can't, or won't, hear them, either. We choose not to hear them. They may be attempting restitution, but we have pulled away. (The person who abused you will more than likely never attempt restitution. We will talk about that soon.)

God gives us an example of a time when a person acts out in anger in Malachi 2:13-16. God refused to hear this person's prayers. Read the passage and pay close attention to verse 16.

In this passage, the man's prayers are not being heard because he is doing what? _____

_____

The word "covering" in this verse is not the same word we learned about from Lamentations. This word is *kacah*, meaning "to fill up hollows, to cover for clothing or secrecy, clad self, close, conceal, cover self, flee to, hide, overwhelm." As you can see, the words have very different meanings. In one case, something is covered in anger to defend or protect it. In the other case, emptiness is being covered with violent anger. In the Malachi verse, the man is using violence to cover the holes inside him. Is this not what we do with our anger when we can't let something go? The hole, the real issue, is not being dealt with. It is fleeing, hiding behind whatever will cover it up. Sometimes that thing is anger. Sometimes the issue is covered with alcohol or drugs, or peacemaking by guilt-taking or downplaying, or sex or food or media or gossip or the hardened shell of portrayed perfection, or any number of things.

Do you use something to "cover" your issues? _____

What specifically do you use? _____

We must understand that nothing and no one can meet all of our needs. We have to learn how to lift those unmet needs up to God and ask Him to satisfy them. We have to learn to ask Him to help us deal with the things that drive us crazy. He is able and more than willing. We have to do this over and over. And when we fail, we have to do it again. Anger gives Satan an opportunity to destroy our relationships. Maybe you have heard verses 26 and 27 of Ephesians 4. "Do not let the sun go down on your _____. Do not give the _____ a _____." The great deceiver will take whatever he can get. Don't let anger fester. You definitely need to step away from the situation long enough to blow off some steam before you say or do something that will hurt the other party involved if we are talking about an issue with a loved one, friend or acquaintance. This verse isn't a call to duke the issue out irresponsibly, but a call to attempt to work the issue out. Sometimes you may need to sleep on it so that you don't give Satan any more ammunition. It is hard to see situations and people clearly when you are harboring anger—especially when we are talking about anger towards people you will most likely never resolve the issue with, like the person who harmed you. This issue is so important that God even tells us that if we have a beef with someone, we have to do our best to clear it up before we come to worship Him (Matt. 5:23, 24).

I know it is one thing to talk about not being mad at the person who hurt you, and another thing altogether to actually feel that way. I did not stop being angry with the people who harmed me until I began to deal first with the abuse and then with myself. As I became secure in the knowledge that I was important to God, and completely loved and cared for by Him, the anger began to fall away. When I trusted God enough to be sure that He would deal with those people according to the truth in His Word, a little more anger melted. The abuse was no longer solely between me and each person. The abuse was now between that person and God, because we all belong to Him.

By being able to release each person and the abuse to God, I was able to look at them not as the monsters who tormented me, but as people who do not know God yet. They will meet God face-to-face one day. Every knee will bow to Him. Every soul will answer to Him. I have no power here to deal with those people, but God does. When they realize the truth of what they did to you, whether it be here on earth or standing before the Maker, they are going to be completely devastated. Only God is capable of changing a person. When you are able to see the person who harmed you as a person who belongs to God, you are winning. You are really beginning to heal.

Sometimes it really helps to write a letter to the person who hurt you. You may have done this in a previous study, but take a few minutes to process what you have learned today and then write them again. Write a letter to each person who abused you. You are going to look over them in small group and then you can throw them away if you want. If you have been holding a grudge against someone else, they get a letter also. You may give it to them in an attempt to make peace, or throw it away after group. Be completely honest. There is no point in doing this study otherwise.

A Serious Lack of Peace: More Issues

Check off all the things a lack of peace in your life can bring:

___ Restlessness ___ Constant reminders ___ Fear ___ Aggression ___ Arguments ___ Lack of sleep ___ Feeling of being out of control ___ Holding grudges ___ Need for control ___ Hopelessness ___ Addictions ___ Perfectionism ___ Bitterness ___ Nightmares/day-mares

All of these can come from a lack of peace in your life. Go back and add any other symptoms you struggle with not listed above.

Now look over the list below of things that can be a "root" to any or all of these outward manifestations of inner turmoil.

___ Abandonment ___ Loss of a loved one ___ Someone did not believe you about the abuse ___ Missing siblings ___ Taking undue blame ___ Believing someone's negative opinion of you ___ Parents who did not love/protect you ___ Lack of personal boundaries ___ Reliance on other "gods" to meet your needs ___ Lack of joy ___ Unmerited feelings of guilt

Do the same with this list. Go over it carefully and check what you deal with; add others if need be. Then, let me share a very sad story with you about a girl I know who held unspeakable guilt in her heart for the loss of a dearly loved brother. I am so sorry that some of you will be able to relate to her situation.

> *Sometimes a truth is so ugly, your entire being rejects it. My brother could not handle the evil attributed to his father. Though we resided in the same house, he was not living the exact same life I was. Our father did not abuse him. Our mother loved and played with him. He was a year and a half older than me, and even though he was mean to me, I still adored him. He left me pretty much alone at our father's house where we lived, but he and mother liked to make me cry when we were at her house. They talked about me, made fun of me, and never let me play with them. Sometimes I hated them, but I always forgave them in the hopes that they would let me in their little circle. I don't know what I did to make them act like that. Why didn't they love me?*
> *When the police came to our father's house one March day, my brother's life began to fall apart.... A knock on the door. "What is this about?" An awful accusation. "Who would say these things!" Two pieces fell from his security. "Why are you taking my sister?" She gets into the black sedan. "What are those handcuffs for?" His father is angry. Life shatters as all the pieces of his life no longer make any sense.*
> *When my brother looked at me that day with anguished questions in his eyes, he was at a crossroads. When he asked me what was going on, and I was not brave enough to tell him the complete truth, he turned and left. He has been gone ever since. A part of my soul has kept him company, though he may never know it. Aside from the abuse of my father, I have suffered the loss of my brother and the hatred of my mother for fifteen years now. She never forgave me for losing him. I should have been braver. Where would my brother be now if I had told him the truth? Is he still alive? I love him as much as I hate him for forgetting me.*

Children should never have to feel like they should have been braver. Hopefully, you caught on to how confused this poor girl was. She had so many different emotions going on she could have opened her own "coat" shop. She loved her mother and brother desperately, even though they were terribly mean to her. In and of itself, there is nothing wrong with her love for her family. But she felt like everything was her fault, even though it was not her fault at all, and there is everything wrong with that! Maybe we should repeat that again. IT WAS NOT HER FAULT. Please write this truth out and put your name in the following blank: The abuse was NOT _____ fault. Children do not have the ability to control situations. They are placed under the care of guardians because they are learning and growing. Children do not have the mental capability to see situations and people clearly. So much of their world is based on emotion, and when those emotions are confused, children are lost. They wander around, trying to make sense of situations they can't possibly understand. They grasp at straws. Since humans are by nature self-centered creatures, they almost always blame themselves. This can also happen to grown women when their hearts are tangled up in a situation.

Have you ever taken on unmerited guilt or shame from something you didn't understand? When? How? _____

_____

_____

_____

Read Job 3:1, 24-26. Can you relate? Has there ever been a time you felt completely lacking in peace? _____

_____

Job is in a terrible state of despair when he speaks here to his friends. Fill in what he says in verse 26: "I have no _____, no _____; I have no _____, but only _____." I think, my dear sisters, we may relate. Please think on one simple fact for a moment. You are not dead, but _____. Alive! You are alive. You have the chance that people who have left this earth without ever knowing that life could be different will never have. Do not think that it is anything less than a miracle that you are still here. No matter what you have suffered, you did not suffer unto death. God has used His power to keep you here because He wants you to know the beauty in a life filled with peace and joy. Do you know how closely linked those two things are in the Bible? Look up Romans 14:17 and Romans 15:13. What do they have in common? _____

_____ Peace and Joy. They go hand in hand. God does not say that peace comes when pain leaves. No, God says peace brings a fearlessness to deal with the situations that cause us pain.

There is another very interesting fact about Job's story. For 35 chapters, God allows Job his questions and heartache. Then, in chapter 38, the Lord speaks to Job. Job 38:1 says, "Then the LORD spoke to Job out of the storm." God does not expect us to live unscathed. He does, however, expect us to listen when He answers. He does want us to see our roles properly. He is God; we are man. Job was finally ready to listen to God, and God called down to him out of the storm that had taken hold of Job's life. Are you ready to listen?

Maybe you don't think God will follow through because no one else did. There is one more testimony to hear today of a young girl who had the same problem. No one would help her. It stole all her trust and peace.

> I refused to go home from school that day. He had caught me before I made it out the door and told me what he was going to do to me when I got home. It was not pretty and I had had enough. It was clear to me that no one was going to believe me. I was going to have to force the hand. When I called to beg my mother to come and get me, she was more excited about the date she had planned for that evening than what her terrified child was trying to tell her. I snuck the phone into the garage to beg her to Come. Get. Me. Now. When I hung up the phone, a part of me wrestled with hysteria. She was my last hope. I had told a girl at school who, in turn, told her mom, but that came to nothing. The police interviewed me in front of the monster who had his hand on my neck the whole time. My lips were sealed that day, but this day, someone was going to listen to me because I was not going home! The counselor at my school sent me home...

Did you ever feel like you were invisible to the entire world, except the abuser? _____

Did you ever wonder if the storm was going to end or swallow you up and could it please just pick one way or the other soon? Have you ever looked at someone living through an extreme situation and seen peace in them? I will never forget how crazy I thought this one elderly couple at church was right after they lost their grown son. They were comforting others after his funeral (?!?). What? How?

Look up Philippians 4:7 and write it out. _____

_____

_____

Look up Ephesians 2:13, 14. Who is our peace? _____
What did he destroy? _____ And look at John 14:27, which reads, "Peace I leave with you; My peace I give you. I do not give as the world gives. Do not let your hearts be troubled and do not be afraid."

Why can Jesus give us peace, you ask? What makes Him qualified? Go to Isaiah 9:6, 7.

What does He carry on his shoulders? _____
What is He called? Prince of _____. Look closely at that word "zeal" at the end of verse 7. That word means "passionate commitment." Our LORD is passionately committed to bringing you peace and joy! Why? He loves you. Why? Because you are His child. Can I hear a Hallelujah?!

Other "gods" in your life, those things you turn to at the first sight of trouble, cannot do what our Savior can do. They will never be able to bring you lasting peace and joy. You may be able to call up a girlfriend and talk till the sun goes down, but eventually you will have to hang up the phone. She has a life also. That drink may give you immediate satisfaction, but it too will be temporary. You can apply this logic to all the things you look to before you look to God. But they did not put the government of the world on their shoulders and carry it for you. They do not have the ability to apply peace like a balm to your soul. Only God can do this.

Do you know that nothing done to, or by, you, can stand in the way of the Lord's promises to you? _____

_____

_____

_____

_____

_____

_____

_____

_____

_____

_____

_____

_____

_____

_____

_____

_____

_____

_____

_____

_____

_____

_____

_____

_____

_____

_____

Right, Wrong, and Still Gray

I hope you are feeling well today. I know that the material in this study can be daunting. Hang in there until the blessing comes. Before you begin today, pray and ask God to renew your strength. Ask for focus and discernment. We are going for total healing here. Boats don't sail very well at half-mast. We are going to dig pretty deeply today, so take a calming breath from the Lord and let's go.

You may have some questions you don't know how to ask. Nearly every single victim of abuse I have spoken with has had questions they felt too embarrassed to ask. We will look at some of these. If there is something in your mind not covered in today's lesson, write it down and bring it with you to group. Do not worry about how the questions will make you look. Worry about how long you have gone without the answers. Now may be the time God gave you to find them.

Did someone try to make you believe you made everything up? Have you ever wondered if you did fabricate a memory?

_____

_____

_____

What? When? _____

_____

_____

It is possible to hear stories and create memories to go along with them. Also, sometimes when an abused person told someone what was going on and that someone did nothing about it, a common reaction would be to make it sound worse in an attempt to get anyone's attention. People will sometimes do things like this when trying to get help. We should not look down on them; we should instead recognize that they are desperately seeking help, and so far they have been denied. Take heart; God will not let any confusion remain in your life if you pray for truth and clarity. Pray the words of John 8:32. "Then you will know the truth, and the truth will set you free." Seek your answers from God alone. Then have confidence that He will give you the strength you need to deal with what comes. You may learn that you misunderstood a situation. But you may learn that you were absolutely correct and someone else was attempting to cover the situation up. You may also uncover parts of your past you had forgotten.

Another question is, "Was it my fault because I looked pretty, sexy, etc.?" Have you been told this? Explain, if so. _____

_____

It is a mother's job to teach young girls how to dress appropriately. This does not mean they can't wear pretty things that look nice on their figures. This just means that the clothing is age-appropriate and modest. This also does not mean that a person has permission to abuse you simply because of the way you look. Some of you did not have mothers to explain why this modesty is necessary. Following are some questions to think about. Maybe you can relate to some. Maybe some are way off the mark. The goal here is to open this subject up for discussion, not to point fingers or judge anyone. There are a lot of things my mother never taught me, and I'm pretty sure I'm not alone there.

Did you receive attention from older boys or men because of your attire? Did you have trouble keeping girlfriends in school? Did boys assume you were the kind of girl who would get physical with them? Did you ever think it was fun to use your attractiveness to get a guy's attention and then attempt to fend him off when he got a little too friendly? Did you have any idea how hard it is for even the best teenage boys to control their bodies and minds when it comes to sexual thoughts? (Again, absolutely no excuse here for abuse; just something to keep in mind when teaching girls how to present themselves.) Did you ever realize that, though the body may look grown at fifteen or sixteen, the mind is not grown until the late twenties? Did anyone ever force you to dress a certain way that made you uncomfortable? Did anyone ever tell you that you were only as good as you were pretty? Did anyone ever teach you that your physical appearance was a gift from God, no matter what you look like? Did anyone ever teach you about the purpose of your virginity?

Write your thoughts down concerning these questions and bring them to group. Now go with me to Genesis 34:1-7. Read and answer the following:

Dinah was the daughter of _____.

What was she doing in verse 1? _____

Who was Shechem? _____

What did he do to Dinah? _____

What was his excuse? _____

_____

What did he tell his father to do? _____

_____

Okay, we need to process this before moving on. Shechem raped Dinah because she was physically beautiful to him. He then tried to declare his love for her. He spoke tenderly to her (v. 3). Dinah was now away from home, violated, and very confused. It makes no matter if Shechem was in love with the girl, although how he could be after one encounter is beyond my comprehension. His tender words to her did not change the fact that he forced her to have sex with him. In the context of that time and culture, he had taken the girl's future from her. No man of Israel would desire to marry a woman without her virginity. This sounds harsh, but let us discover, some for the first time, what is so special about a girl's virginity.

Blood covenants are woven throughout God's Word, symbolizing the creation of bonds meant never to be broken. We see this with the covenant made between God and Abraham. Genesis 17 teaches us about the covenant of circumcision. We see it again in Leviticus 16, when God teaches the necessity of a blood sacrifice upon an altar for the atonement of man's sin. Lifeblood was the cost of sin. In Exodus 24, when the Israelites returned to God, the covenant was confirmed with blood. The ultimate covenant of Christ's sacrifice upon the cross was for all mankind. Christ's blood flows freely for the covering of all our mistakes. A covenant, once accepted, is never able to be broken. At least that is how covenants are designed to be.

Now let's learn about the beautifully designed covenant for marriage. When a woman has intercourse for the first time, blood from her hymen (a small layer of soft tissue) covers the act. Marriage is a bond never meant to be broken between man and woman. Go to Matthew 19:3-9. Jesus teaches here what is taught in the Old Testament about a man and a woman becoming of one flesh when they are married. He teaches that God has joined the couple together and the cords of that bond should not be unraveled.

Turn to Ephesians 5:22-33. This passage tells couples how they are to reverently treat each other in marriage. What does verse 22 say women should do? _____

_____ The word "submit" here does not mean to be a doormat or a slave. It means to respect your man for the role he has in your life. It means to honor him, support him and take care of his needs. It means to listen to his direction as the protector and provider of the family. In short, you could look at it this way: God is saying "Work together because you are now one." The society we live in keeps trying to tear down this format of marriage. A woman's choice of submission to her husband is becoming an idea of the dark ages, the very act insinuating weakness. But is a man weak when he follows God's direction in marriage?

Write out verse 28: _____

_____ Husbands have a heavy charge as well. Marriage was made to be a connection so powerful it would last a lifetime. God supplied the blood in virginity to bind a covenant of marriage. Teach this gift to your daughters, and to your friends who don't have mothers who will teach them.

Going back to Dinah's story, we can see that the taking of a woman's virginity without her consent is nothing new. This is truly a devastating ordeal. What is taken in the act of rape goes beyond the physical realm and into the very soul of the female. My dear sister, I am speaking directly to you. Please listen closely. I would look you straight in the eye right now if I could. I know your desperate darkness. I know your black hole, your tempest, your nightmare, your crawling skin, your unimaginable pain, and your questions. I know your loss and your cage. My deepest prayer is that you may know my sunshine. God heals. God gives back what Satan takes. The enjoyment of sexual intimacy is not meant to be a one-sided affair. We will study a day on this topic, but today, hear the voice of a friend who knows. We are not lost. We do not remain defiled. We are still beautiful and precious. Someone will still be able to love us and touch us with desire and kindness. There is healing from rape and abuse. You will be whole.

You may ask, "Have I also lost the blessing God provides through blood covenant in marriage if I have lost my virginity out of wedlock?" Good question. Here is your answer: No. You have not lost what God wanted you to share with your future husband if your innocence was taken. God does not work that way. Never does He say, "You're on your own here, so fix things the best way you can." God can and does create lasting bonds in the covenant of marriage through any situation. You are / will be worthy of your husband. You are / will be free to be his wife in every aspect. You must choose to embrace that truth.

Even if you were not forced to have intercourse with your abuser, you probably still have a deep sense of a loss of innocence. The abuse may have opened the door to your becoming sexually active. This is usually what happens. You may have willingly lost your virginity without understanding the details of a marriage covenant. If there is one thing I have repeatedly heard from women who have similar backgrounds, it is, "I wish I had known what my virginity meant in God's eyes." But take heart—your past choices do not condemn your future blessings from God unless you allow them to. In this way, you have lost just as much as our other sisters. It does not matter if the abuse happened one time or many times; the resulting confusion is the same. In Dinah's story, her family was enraged. They thought along the lines of protecting and avenging her. Although her brothers made terrible mistakes in their anger, bringing further destruction, they were not the ones who abused her. Some of you were not so lucky. A family member or close friend is more often to blame for abuse than a stranger. Life can seem unbearable at times. I would agree to defeat if there were only one side of this coin. However, we must not forget the other side; the side that has already claimed our lives for their team. When nothing else on earth makes sense, cling to the knowledge that you belong to God. Tomorrow we will look at what you really mean to Him.

Write out every word of Ezekiel 34:15, 16. Pray it. Claim it. You are of His flock. He is searching for you. He will bind you up and strengthen you mind, body, and soul. _____

_____

_____

_____

_____

_____

_____

_____

_____

_____

_____

_____

_____

Now pray, and I will pray with you, for God to show you He means business.

A Worthy Intercessor

Without a deep understanding of why Christ is worthy to be our Savior, it can be hard to look upon His strength as something we can, or even desire to, pull from. It is like attempting to trust a stranger to keep in confidence your every thought. It is like asking that same stranger to never leave you. Could you walk up to someone you have never met and say, "Okay, Mr. . . . um, what's your name again? I am going to put my life in your hands; do with me as you will." That sounds crazy, because it is! You share unique bonds with people you know and love. There is an automatic lowering of fences when in the presence of trusted friends. When they pray for you, you take comfort. Their prayers are trusted; therefore, they give you strength.

Christ became a man in order to become your trusted friend. Christ, fully man. Christ, fully God. He was sent here to intercede for every created soul. He left this world a victor and has never put down His charge. We cannot understand this deed without understanding how much it cost Him. His sacrifice was no simple thing. While He was suffering unimaginable anguish, do you have any idea where His mind was? I can't wait to tell you this if you do not already know. His mind, in the midst of the greatest struggle on earth, was on you. Let that speak directly to your heart and go with me to a handful of moments after the Last Supper and before the cross. Turn to John 17. Take a moment to ask God to give you the vision of an eyewitness. Ask Him to let this scene unfold in your mind as if you were one of the disciples standing beside Jesus. Listen to the soil at your feet displace as you walk on it. Color everything you see with moonlight. Ask God to allow you to walk with your Savior, along a well beaten path, into a favorite garden.

Read John 17:3, 11, 19-23 (This is a beautiful chapter if you have time to read all of it). Jesus is praying to His Father. These are some of the last things we will hear Him say, so by that fact alone, they are very important. If you had only hours left in your life, where would you go? What would you say? Who would you say it to?

_____

_____

_____

Fill in these blanks pulled from Jesus's heart for those He loves: (v. 20, 21) "My _____ is not for them [the disciples] alone. I pray also for _____ ____ ____ _____ ___ through their _____, that all of them may be one, Father, just as ____ are in ____ and ____ am in _____. May _____ also be in _____ so that the _____ may believe that _____ have sent _____." (v. 23) "May they be brought to complete unity to let the world _____ that you _____ me and have _____ them even as you have loved me."

Now let us walk with Him deeper into the garden where He shows us just how human His fully-man self was. Breathe in the scent of wild vegetation and take a seat on the cool night ground. Turn to, and read, Mark 14:32-42. Take notice of some important points.

Mark 14:33 says Jesus took three of the disciples with Him to sit and keep watch over Him while He prayed. He was deeply _____ and _____.

Mark 14:34 shows us the physical and mental state Christ was in during this leg of His journey. Remember that He came to earth for a purpose and He was about to face the hardest part of His mission. He knew every single thing that was going to happen to Him from that moment on. He knew every tear of His flesh, every drop of spittle in His eye, and every person who would betray and mock Him. He was praying for strength to die in one of the most awful ways human minds ever devised.

In Mark 14:36 Jesus calls out from the pit of his being to His Father. He calls Him, literally, "Daddy," beseeching God with the most endearing title children can call their father. Then Jesus asks God to choose another way to accomplish His will, if it is possible. In verse 36 Jesus says, "Take this cup from me." Go back a few steps from the garden, back into the upper room, to see what Jesus is talking about.

In Luke 22:20, "This cup" passed around to the disciples is literally the third cup of the Passover celebration, the cup representing the redemption of God's people. If you look at Exodus 6:6, 7, you will learn the meaning of the four cups of wine the Israelites drink at the Passover meal each year. (I have recapped these symbols and promises in the table below for you.) They do this in remembrance of the promises God made to His people when He brought them out of Egyptian slavery. (This Truth is explained quite nicely in Beth Moore's Jesus, the One and Only Bible study.) Jesus' death, His sacrifice, was going to be the final, ultimate offer of redemption to God's people. Never again would anyone need to sacrifice an animal on an altar to pay for the atonement of their sins, and the opportunity to have a personal relationship with God was forever solidified with "this cup."

The Symbol	What the Symbol Represents	God's Promise to His People
The first cup:	The cup of Sanctification.	I will bring you out from under the yoke of the Egyptians.
The second cup:	The cup of Deliverance.	I will free you from being slaves to them.
The third cup:	The cup of Redemption.	I will redeem you with an outstretched arm and with mighty acts of judgment.
The fourth cup:	The cup of In-Gathering.	I will take you as My own people, and I will be your God.

Jesus came to earth to fulfill the third cup. His heart belonged to you, but His physical body was desperately rejecting the way in which you would be able to claim the promise of redemption with one final sacrifice: His human death. I believe God allowed Him to suffer so heavily for two reasons: (1) in order that He would be able to relate to our physical and mental trials; and (2) sacrifice that costs nothing means nothing. Go with me to 2 Samuel 24:22-24.

Araunah was offering King David to take anything he wanted from his possessions and offer it to the LORD as a sacrifice. Araunah says, "Here, take this freely and may the LORD accept your offerings." But David understood a little bit about his God in this area.

What does David say to Araunah in verse 24? _____

_____

David knew that the truth and power of a sacrifice lay in what it cost a man deep inside. He basically said, "If it does not cost me anything, then it does not mean anything to me or to my God."

Christ understood this very simple, yet extremely deep, truth, also. That is why the next thing Christ prayed in Mark 14:36 was, "Yet not what _____ will, but what _____ will." God could have skipped any step Christ took, but you meant more to Him than physical and mental pain. You meant more to Him than letting evil touch Him and being separated from His Father until He defeated Satan. Christ had never been apart from God up to this point. He was with God when the world was formed, and, as a human, Christ had never sinned. Sin is what separates us from God.

Imagine being ripped in two. In one of the greatest mysteries of heaven, God, Christ, and the Holy Spirit are one. Picture the element of water in your mind. You know full well that H2O can be three distinctly different substances in the form of liquid water, gaseous steam, and solid ice. The Holy Trinity is just like that, each uniquely different but all the same element. When Christ allowed ALL the sin that ever had entered, and ever would enter, this world to completely cover Him on the cross, God had to separate Himself from Himself.

I know this is hard to understand, but God the Father will not be in the presence of sin. Sin is the antithesis to all that God is. That is why Adam and Eve had to leave the garden. That is why Christ had to shed His lifeblood to redeem us from the choices we make.

We cannot have a one-on-one relationship with God apart from the redemption Christ made available to every person who has sinned.

When you decide that the truth God teaches is a truth you believe in, then, and only then, nothing can take you from your Maker's hand. And please remember that God's love is not conditional. Once you are redeemed, you can't become unredeemed. When you mess up after becoming a Christ-follower, you don't lose redemption, you lose the closeness of God's presence in your life until you come back to Him.

I can't even imagine allowing someone else's sin to touch me. When I think of putting a psychopath's sin upon my body like Christ did, it makes me sick. In this light, I can understand why He was praying for the third cup to be taken from Him (aside from the extreme physical pain He endured, of course). We sometimes fool ourselves into believing that there are different levels of sin to God—how is rape the same as a lie? How is murder even close to a lack of forgiveness? They are not the same by any means, but they are written on the same page. In medical terms, they are in the same family of illness. When a person chooses to do something that causes harm, that is sin. That separates you from God. Acceptance of Christ's choices for you knits you and God back together.

Let's not miss a tender moment in the garden between Father and Son. Mark does not record this event, but Luke does. Turn to Luke 22:43. Write this one out: _____

_____

_____

In a dark hour, God sends His angel to strengthen Christ. Not alone do we walk this earth. Never alone do we face trials we have no idea how to conquer. God would not remove the trial, but He did send help.

Jesus was praying for you as He went to the garden of Gethsemane. He was praying for you as He allowed man to beat Him over and over. He was praying for you, individually, to come to know truth as His eyes looked upon the cross those soldiers laid Him on. As the nails drove through His flesh; as the blood poured out of His body to the mingled sounds of jeers and wails.

What could have held Him to His course when at any moment He could have thrown off His human flesh? The thought of you going through this life without Him kept Him there.

Christ did not stop praying for you after He died and rose again. His earthly job was finished, but yours isn't. What does Hebrews 7:25 say Christ is always doing? _____

_____

I can just see Him there, standing over the crib of a child who hears no earthly lullaby. I can hear His prayers for that child as sweet melodies sung over them. I get it when people go out of their way to do kind things for strangers with no thought of what might be in it for them. What do you think is happening when a door suddenly opens up to an opportunity you never thought would come your way? This is the simple, everlasting kindness of our Savior. I know—I KNOW—that He prays for our strength when we stand at a crossroads. With our ear turned to Him, we turn right. Deaf to Him, we will turn left again and again.

I hope that today you were able to see your Savior in a new light. I hope that His tenderness was able to shine clear and bold off of these pages. I pray you recognized His unimaginable strength and power.

Was there ever a time someone was nice to you for no apparent reason? _____

Have you ever felt God's clear direction in a specific situation?

_____

Have you ever witnessed the power of honest prayer from a group of friends? _____

Did you know that Christ still lives to intercede for you?

_____

Do you believe that Christ was with you when you thought you were completely alone? _____

Not a Desolate Woman!

God's Promise: He will search for you, He will bind you up. (Ezek. 34:16)
He will give you NEW strength. (Isa. 40:31)

Do you believe this? _____

Why? Why not? _____

_____

_____

Satan's Lie: You Are Alone. You are weak. You do not matter. Judgment is yours.

Do you believe this? _____

Why? Why not? _____

_____

_____

The Account of Tamar

This week, we are really going to examine the promises God makes to all His children in Ezekiel 34. We first glanced at this promise on day four of last week. I pray that you noticed the roles of God and man correctly in those heartwarming passages. God is the pursuer and man is the one being searched for. The problem we often run into as physical creatures is that we have a hard time finding what we cannot see in a tangible form. However, God has no problem finding us. Nothing is hidden from His sight. Hebrews 4:13 has been of great comfort to many who have wondered if God really can see everything. What does this verse say? _____

_____

_____

We will also look at the strength God promises to give us when we can't go on otherwise. Think back on our last lesson when God sent the angel to Jesus in the midst of one of His darkest hours. God did not remove the trial, but He did renew Christ's strength. There are a staggering amount of professed Christians who believe and teach that the Christian life is one absent of peril. This is not so! God never promises us that life will be easy and we will be blessed with material wealth, good health, and only nice people around us. Sometimes, when I am listening to messages of this nature (which I like to call "fluff and stuff"), I wonder if they ever read those Bibles they carry in their *left* hands?

Today, we are going to look at Tamar, a beautiful daughter of King David. She started out a princess; she ended her life as a desolate woman. We are going to break this story down, scene-by-scene, because of the vast amount of mistakes made throughout the situation. Sometimes, the easiest way to learn something is to pick a similar ordeal apart. Our goal here is to look at each point of Tamar's story, and identify what went wrong where. It can be easy to think that the Bible is composed of fictional characters, especially when recounting the Old Testament. Do not allow yourself that distance. These people breathed. Their stories were recorded so that all of creation after them could see how God worked in their lives. Let us not waste this gift. God does not wish us to live the remainder of our lives as desolate women. God desires us to thrive. God desires us to not just press on, but to be able to go on in peace and joy as wonderful displays of His glory. I wish it could have been so for Tamar.

Turn to 2 Samuel 13 and read the entire chapter first, so you can get the whole picture; then we need to break this story down. Let's start by identifying the main people involved:

> *Tamar*—Virgin daughter of King David, full sister to Absalom, half-sister to Amnon
>
> *Absalom*—Full brother of Tamar, half-brother of Amnon, son of David
>
> *Amnon*—Firstborn son of King David, half-brother to Tamar and Absalom, in line for the throne after David
>
> *Jonadab*—Cousin and friend to Amnon
>
> *David*—King of Israel, Father to Tamar, Absalom, and Amnon

Today's focus will be on verses 1-9.

Verses 1, 2: Amnon wants to have physical relations with his half-sister Tamar. He becomes obsessed with her because he cannot have her. Mosaic Law forbids the sexual relations of any brother and sister (Lev. 18:9, 11). Although in Old Testament times we clearly see that families often married within distant relations of their own tribe, incest was never permissible to God. The whole chapter of Leviticus 18 goes down a long list specifically writing out the law concerning this subject. Does this fact give you comfort in some way? _____

Verses 3, 4: Enter Jonadab, Amnon's friend and cousin. Blatantly defined as a shrewd and deceitful man, Jonadab would be very happy to see trouble in the king's house. See how he cleverly jumps on the opportunity to feed into Amnon's feelings of entitlement? Jonadab is not unaware of the fact that the firstborn son of royalty normally gets whatever he wants. (As parents, we should be very mindful of how much we spoil our children and just who their friends are. If we are not paying attention to them, they will find someone who will, no matter how many gadgets and toys they are given.)

Notice how Amnon tries to separate the family ties between himself and Tamar by calling her not his sister but his brother's sister. He is trying to rationalize a way into getting what he wants and make it sound less wrong. But, see, Amnon knows it is wrong. They all know they are wrong; that's why they hide. Take special note that in verse 4 Amnon also confuses love with lust. Do you understand the difference between the two? _____

_____

_____

Look here at some of the differences between love and lust. Where lust requires an *immediate satisfaction,* love *waits patiently* for what it wants. Lust vanishes upon temporary fulfillment; love *grows* stronger with fulfillment. Lust *demands* its own way, sometimes very harshly, and usually without consideration of what anyone else wants. Love has vastly different qualities. Love is kind and *selfless.* Within the context of marriage, physical and emotional love can, and should often be, very exciting. The point we need to grasp here is that real love always gives and lust *always takes.*

Did someone profess love to you while they hurt you? _____

_____

Did their contradicting words and actions cause confusion about what love really meant to you? _____

Verses 5-7: Amnon plays on the concern of his father. David is blind to the plot Amnon and Jonadab have devised. I doubt seriously that even in the farthest reaches of David's mind would he have been suspecting that his son was plotting to rape his daughter. To a parent, some things are just ludicrous to think about, even if a shadow of truth haunts them, so David sends for Tamar to tend to his "ill" son. All players here, aside from the plotters, are unsuspecting of Amnon's motives.

Verses 8, 9: Tamar is simply doing what has been asked of her. Did she have any idea these would be her last sane moments? Can't we just freeze time right here! Oh, that we could have rushed in and changed this whole scene...

Was there a time before your abuse that you felt whole and happy? _____

Do you believe you will ever feel that way again? Or maybe for the first time ever? _____

Can you see ANY possible fault in Tamar at this moment?

_____

We need to stop here and allow God to help us focus on the points brought up today. The Tamar we meet today is a lovely young woman. She is titled and beautiful. She is who all the peasant girls pretend to be in their fairytale games on hot afternoons as they are doing their chores. Tamar is the young woman life has not yet worked too harshly on. She walks around with her head lifted, comfortable in who she is.

There is one sensitive topic I am feeling led to bring out here. I have heard many, many, women say that in an attempt to fend off future abuse, they have allowed themselves to gain weight. One dear woman told me that she felt like the weight was her only protection. She said when she was thin, men would notice her physical form and she was so afraid they would be filled with the same desires her abusers were. Can you relate to this woman in any way? How so?

_____

_____

_____

God did not make us all to be supermodels; thank goodness, because we would deplete the world's supply of make-up and hairspray! God did, however, create us to be comfortable within our own skin. Weight or lack of weight is not what will protect you from evil-minded people. Women from all walks of life have suffered abuse. God made the physical part of you in such a way that your beauty is really seen when you know that you are loved. And just in case no one has ever told you this: You are beautiful. You are a dearly loved daughter of the King. He made you to exact specifications. Tomorrow, we will walk a little farther with Tamar, but today, try to imagine what it would be like to feel comfortable and confident in your own skin.

Did breaking the first part of Tamar's story down like this help you see any specific aspects of your situation differently? Which ones and how so? _____

_____

_____

_____

_____

_____

_____

_____

Lord, sometimes we feel so much at the mercy of those who seem bigger than us. They have great power to harm smaller things. Remind us, Lord, that when we face these things, we face them for a reason. We face them with You. We face them because, and only because, we will be able to overcome them. Amen.

Act Two

Yesterday we looked at the calm before the storm. We left Tamar making some bread for an "ill" family member. Go back to 2 Samuel 13 with me. This will be a difficult day of study. Take a moment to pray and ask God to highlight the truth He wants to show you in His word. Ask God to help you remember where confusion came into your life. In your journal, write out the specific things about your story that really confused you. Was it something someone said? Was it a way in which the abuse was covered up? Was it how you were looked at or how you felt after? Even if you were not raped, you were still abused and much of the story dynamics can apply to you. Deep breath... Read verses 9-14 and then we will break the story down like we did yesterday.

Verses 9-11: There is a terrible moment here when the realization dawns on Tamar that she is trapped. Do you see how easily this happens? If you have ever wondered how abuse could have ever happened to you, look here. Look how innocent the plot appeared to be. Look how devious the evil players were. Look how no one, except the plotters, realized what was going on until it was too late. Have you ever wondered how no one realized what was happening to you? _____

One adolescent girl wrote something that breaks me. The note she slipped me read: *Why couldn't they hear me? I did try to tell them. Why couldn't anybody see? Can evil hide that well?*

Take a few moments to ask God to reveal any animosity in your heart. These are the things we are here for, doing this study, attempting to work through. Do you harbor any hate or anger toward someone who should have seen what was happening, but for whatever reason did not? _____

_____

Moving forward is not possible without this knowledge and honesty. You may not have to tell them how you feel, but you need to tell yourself and God so that this can be worked through. The pain can turn to resentment and resentment of one person's actions is easily generalized to cover completely unrelated people and situations. Looking back, have you ever punished one person for another's actions? How so? An example would be something like: "I could not trust so-and-so; therefore I cannot trust you." Or, "I never had control over anything, so I HAVE to have control now." "If I don't have control, things will go all wrong because I am the only one who can be trusted." _____

_____

_____

Verse 12: Tamar tries to reason with the unreasonable. Amnon is blinded by his lust. He must, at all cost, control the situation in order to get what he wants. Christ tells us that wicked people cannot understand the truth. They turn from truth to satisfy the selfishness that consumes them. Look up John 3:19, 20. What did these evil men love instead of light? _____ Why? (v. 19) _____ Why? (v. 20) _____

Can we reiterate that last point? People who are knowingly doing things wrong will not listen to the truth because they are afraid their deeds will be seen, and they will get into trouble or have to stop whatever they are doing. It's a defense mechanism of the worst sort to simply refuse to acknowledge the truth.

Verse 13: "What about me!" Tamar is pleading for her life with Amnon, but abusers *do not* see past their own desires. Victims are left to pick up the tatters of whatever is left of our lives. Thankfully, if we allow Him, God can pull us out of the deepest waters. When no one else thinks of what will happen to you after the terrible things you went through, God does. Hear the voice of this young woman who suffered repeated rapes at the hand of someone who should have protected her. She thought she was alone, but one day she realized where her strength came from.

She writes in third person form.

> "He tried to break her; he took everything she never knew she had away from her. He threw her down on a cold, stale floor, had his fun, and then just left her there. She would never even resemble a child again. A musty garage smell would take it from her. The sound of a door locking would steal it from her. His laughter would shatter her into razor-sharp pieces that she would sweep up off that cold floor and put into her pocket because she would be damned if she left any of them there. She would never believe his lies about what was and was not love. She hurt, she bled, she cried, she tried to run and she got very, very, mad. But she did not break. She did not break. Where this strength came from, she never knew. She didn't even care for a while. Life was about survival. Then one day when she could breathe again, she wondered, "Where did that strength come from?" And gentle as a night breeze off the ocean, God whispered, "**It came from Me.**"

In Ezekiel 34:16, God says He will bind up the injured and
_____ the weak. Philippians 4:13 says:

_____

Our strength comes from God, even when we have yet to realize it.

Take a moment to read Psalm 18:16-19. What does this say to you personally? _____

_____

Are you still waiting for the rescue, or have you already taken hold of His hand? Are you dipping your toes in the water, not ready or willing to let go completely? Do you know that no one else is strong enough to pull you into a "spacious place?"

_____

Have you tried to seek healing from someone other than God?

_____

How has that worked out? _____

Verse 14: "But he refused to listen to her . . ." Amnon could hear nothing other than the raging of his pent-up lust. Do not miss the highlighted fact here that he was stronger than she. I think this point is brought out to remind us that we are not equally matched against the abuser. Why do you think abusers go for much younger and/or weaker targets? Had we been on level footing, they would not have been able to do what they did.

Many people who suffer feel as if they do not have the strength to deal with what has been placed before them. Physical and mental weakness can breed defeat, or anger—or, worse yet, it can steal your faith. God does not expect you to be some kind of mighty superwoman, immune to any hardships. He did not weave impenetrable armor into your flesh. What He did create when He knit you together in perfect precision was a vessel capable of being filled with His Spirit. Flesh with the ability to call upon the Maker. He provided the means for an open communication system where no strong wind, or raging thunderstorm, or person who refuses to hear your pleas, could lay down the lines between you. When you feel weak and He promises you a new strength, He means to give it to you. Turn with me to Isaiah 40:27-31.

When we feel as if our trials are not looked upon by our God, strength fails us. Verse 27 asks God, "Can't you see me, LORD?" Then the next four verses were penned in answer to that S.O.S.

We may grow tired and weary, but does God ever reach that point? _____

Verse 28 meets the questioning heart with a powerful answer. What is that answer? _____

_____

_____

When up against something that terrifies you, it is natural to feel too small. You are human, subject to human limits upon your strength. That is why God is always a prayer away. He gives strength to the weary and increases your ability to stand in the face of adversity (v. 29-31). The key to attaining this strength rests on one little word in verse 31. Please fill in this blank: "But those who _____ in the LORD will renew their strength." Place your hope in the LORD. He is so much bigger than you will ever understand—until you stand before His throne in stark contrast to His mighty power.

One more gift He gives to us is mentioned in verse 31. When we place our hope in Him, we not only get strength, but we get to soar! God asks us to make a choice, and then He does all the rest in abundance.

Close today by asking God to apply some of that incredible strength to you now. What are your weakest areas? What are your biggest questions? You were meant to soar in God's unfailing strength. His is the power alone to get you through the worst of this life. _____

_____

_____

_____

_____

_____

_____

_____

_____

_____

From Lust to Hate

S ome ugly truths about abuse will be uncovered today. We are slowly trudging through Tamar's story because it contains so many points that need to be opened up for discussion. Today, we will look at verses 15-19. I hope that yesterday you began to understand how easy it is for evil-minded people to prey on others. I also pray (p-r-a-y) that you began to realize where your strength comes from. God will not leave us to deal with other people's choices on our own. His compassion does not even allow us to deal with our own choices alone, if we also bring those issues to Him. He is our Father and He loves us incomprehensibly, unconditionally, and powerfully.

Reread 2 Samuel 13:15-19 to refresh your memory.

Verse 15: A shift occurs in verse 15 as lust turns to hate, revealing the perpetrator's true motive. Amnon slakes his lust, then has to figure out how to deal with his mistake. Once the deed is done, the reality of the situation stands out. He chooses a common tactic of the immature, selfish man: he shifts blame. He treats Tamar as if she had done something wrong.

Did the person who abused you tell you that it was your fault?

_____

Did you believe them? Why? _____

_____

Did someone else try to tell you that the abuse was your fault?

_____

Did you believe them? _____

This can be one of the most damaging and hurtful things victims have to deal with. The blame has to go somewhere, and it is commonly attached to the weakest party involved. There are some situations when one parent will blame a child for the other family member's or parent's abuse. This is so *wrong*. There is no excuse for this behavior. The only thing I can think of is that the parent is in a state of total lockdown—fear that causes one or more of several reactions: (1) Blind denial: I will not look at it and it will go away. (Yeah, okay. That never works. People just get hurt more this way.) (2) Total revulsion that they could have married someone so sick and evil (self-preservation that says it must be someone else's fault). (3) Complete inability to deal with the situation—how will the abuser react when confronted? (4) Worry about what others will think (not wanting the abuse to be seen by anyone). (5) Not having a clue as to how to talk to the one who was abused.

Does any of this relate to your situation? _____

Have you experienced this blame-shifting in other ways? _____ I am going to say this as many times as it takes for it to become reality in the marrow of your life: the abuse was not your fault. In all reality, Amnon was saying, "Get this situation away from me so I don't have to deal with the repercussions of my actions." Abusers will stoop to all levels in order to save their own skin.

Verses 16-19: Tamar tries to salvage whatever she has left. She begs Amnon to see the situation he has put her in. Now that she is no longer a virgin, her chances of marriage are gone. Her life has been thrown up into the air. Suspended there, she sees the cliff Amnon is about to throw her off of, and she clings to solid ground for dear life. However, he callously tosses her over, anyway, and then he locks the door behind her. In her shame, Tamar tears the ornamented robe she wears that displays her status as a virgin daughter of the king; she no longer feels worthy of this position. She can no longer claim the honor she has been blessed with by birthright. In one afternoon's time, everything has been taken from her.

Was the shame Tamar felt rightfully hers to bear? _____

Who should have carried this shame? _____

I hope you wrote Amnon in that space. Shame is a fruit of sin just as kindness is a fruit of love. The sin Amnon committed bore shame that, in truth, rested on Amnon. Tamar felt this shame because Amnon blamed everything on her, and in her devastation, she was totally lost. Did you ever feel shame from your abuse? _____ Dear one, this shame does not belong to you. If you have not already given it back to the person who abused you, it is time to do so now. Pray for strength and wisdom. Ask God to help you put the fruit of this sin back where it belongs.

Rape/abuse takes nearly everything from its victim. Life will never be the same. People will never be the same. There's a before, and then there's an after; after can be extremely daunting. Life can take us places that no one should ever have to go. We cannot sit around and wallow in the place we have been, no matter how awful that place was. I can tell you this from experience. I hope never to look into eyes that have seen what my eyes have seen, but I know you are out there. I survived and healed for you to know that total healing is possible. I never thought I would reclaim even a single piece of what was taken from me, but God has other plans for us. He desires for us to know peace, joy, love, and laughter in this life. When we come into His light and ask to know His will, He begins to restore us. The process is long and painful, but so is a life lived in the past. The difference is that one holds hope and one does not.

Turn to Matthew 6:33. In this passage, from verses 25 to 34, Jesus is teaching about worry. We worry about a lot of things, don't we? What does verse 33 tell us we should worry about above all else?

Verse 33 tells us that if we will seek first the kingdom of God, we will be given everything else we need. Basically, this can be boiled down to a few simple truths:

1. **If you seek first to please yourself, then you will only receive yourself.**

   I am asking this as a sister, with no judgment: Do you use self-ishness as a cloak of protection? Maybe no one ever considered you, so you had to put yourself first from then on? _____

_____

Do you have a driving need to control all situations so that no one will mess things up? Or so that no one will ever hurt you again? Or because you only really trust yourself to do things correctly?

_____

Have you ever found yourself thinking you were better than someone because you haven't made some of the choices they have?

_____

2. **If you seek to live in the past, you will never know the riches of the future.**
    Do you have a need to recount parts, or all, of your story to anyone who will listen? Maybe no one ever listened before, and you are stuck in the "no one sees me" mode? _____

    _____

    Have you ever felt like the sympathy you received from sharing your pain was the only connection you could get with people?

    _____

3. **If you seek first to harbor anger and hatred towards someone, you will never know the freedom of forgiveness that you will receive.**
    Can you see how holding onto anger keeps you tied to the person you hate? _____

    Do you know that forgiving someone does not mean you think what they did is okay? _____

    Did you know that when you forgive, it really means you have chosen to move on? _____

4. **If you seek first to know God, you will be blessed beyond measure. Put your trust in Him even if you only have a drop of it left.**
    Locate Psalm 10 in the Word. I love this psalm because of the last two verses. They were such a comfort to me when I was trying to decide who was bigger—God or the abusers. If we are

honest with ourselves, I think we have all asked questions like: "Why do they get away with doing bad things?" "How can I put my trust in God when evil runs all over this earth?" "When do they have to face what they did to me?" We are going to study God's judgment on day five, but for today, rest in the knowledge that you are seen. Read Psalm 10. Pay special attention to verses 12-18.

Write out what verse 14 speaks to you: _____

_____

Write out whatever verses 17 and 18 speak to you: _____

_____

No two situations of abuse are the same. However, there are many common issues that are born of abuse. We can go over lists of side effects and statistics of all sorts, but what we really need to do is know that we are not alone. Are you ready to move on? If not, ask God to reveal to you whatever it is that is holding you back.

_____

_____

_____

_____

_____

_____

_____

_____

_____

_____

DAY 4

Desolation

On day one, we talked about how the stories in the Bible were recorded so that we could see how God worked in those people's lives. I would not be surprised if you have already asked where God was in Tamar's life. I think the lesson today will help clear this point up. The answer lies with Absalom. We'll focus on Absalom's choices in this chapter, and a few chapters after, for very important reasons. People need godly help and direction in their lives at times when nothing makes sense. We, as members of the body of Christ, can either hand them a paddle to row with or a stone to drag them down. We will never know what happens with each individual person as they stand before the throne of our Lord. What we can see is the state in which a person lives here, and "here" matters a great deal. Sadly, when Tamar desperately needed a paddle, she was handed a stone.

We will visit 2 Samuel 13 one more time. Read the last three verses again.

Verse 20: Now we come to a fate even worse than the original deed provides. Absalom, Tamar's full brother, finds her and discovers what happened. Instead of bringing the incident into the light and demanding that it be dealt with, Absalom tells Tamar to keep quiet. Keep Quiet! That's like saying, "You are not worth rescuing." That statement is a death sentence to Tamar. Then, he tells her not to take it to heart. Sweeping the issue under the rug only destroys the rug from the inside out. Indeed, she took the rape to heart, and to body, and to mind! Absalom's advice to not make a big deal of the issue is what led Tamar to live the rest of her life in desolation. Tamar went to someone she trusted, and he silenced her.

To see a woman or child live this way is heartbreaking. One woman shared with me how her husband would sit in his recliner and watch television while she sat curled up by the back door crying her heart out. His callousness was born of an inability to help her, so he attempted to simplify the situation. His tactic was for her to "just get over it already." It was not a big surprise when they divorced.

Absalom responded to Tamar's suffering this way because he wanted to take revenge upon Amnon himself. Absalom was consumed with hatred for what Amnon did to Tamar, but he dealt with it in such a way that cost his sister her healing. Absalom spent the next eleven years of his life plotting revenge against his family.

Did a similar situation happen to you where someone told you to keep quiet about the abuse? _____

How long was it before you could tell anyone what happened to you? _____

Did you get the help you needed? Were you protected from the abuser? _____

Do you see how Absalom's reaction was wrong? _____

Do you think there is ever a situation where the abuse should be keep secret? _____

Verse 21: David was furious as well, but he did not make one movement to care for Tamar, either. David did nothing. The penalty for Amnon's sin was that he be cut off from the entire family (Lev. 20:17). David did not want to deliver this judgment to the heir to his throne. David also probably felt the weight of his past choices upon him. He had repeatedly taken wives and concubines, showing an open display of sexual excess to any little eyes watching. This excess was against the law he was supposed to be upholding. Looking at this, we can see that Amnon learned sexual impurity from living in the palace. David also repeatedly shows a severe lack of wise parenting. These pieces put together helped lead them all into this situation. The guilt he felt for his part in the ordeal must have been staggering. God forgave David for the sins he committed, but He did not withhold the hand of consequence.

Verse 22: Although Absalom clearly loved his sister, he did not demand action, either. He quietly fumed and hated. When a situation is not *immediately* dealt with, nothing good comes of it. It never simply goes away like it never happened. When abuse is "kept quiet," healing will not follow. We are incapable of fixing ourselves. The damage is too deep. We are not capable of sorting out the truth from the lies unless we are taken by the hand and walked through the truth. We must be able to travel through it as many times as is needed in order for the confusion and pain inside us to be cleared. It is never going to just go away. Time does not heal all wounds. There has to be someone who says, "pour your heart out, tell me everything that happened, let me look at you." Do not cover yourself in shame that does not belong to you and sit in a state of loss any longer. God has sent you to this study so that you do *not* live the rest of your life the way Tamar lived hers. You are not meant for desolation. Something that is desolate is devoid of inhabitants, deserted, a wasteland.

Has the abuse you suffered left you feeling this way at times?

_____

When does it seem to be worse?_____

_____

Did you ever feel like no one saw you, even if they were looking right at you? _____

One woman explained her feelings of desolation this way:

> *It was this constant, driving demand inside me. Look at me. See me. Know me. Want to know me. Want me. It was a deep sense of wanting desperately for someone to KNOW me. To UNDERSTAND me. I felt so lost, insignificant, and empty. I felt like an invisible stranger everywhere I went. It got to the point where I even pushed anyone away who tried to get to know me, because I was certain they would eventually see me as insignificant, also. Everyone else ignored my heart, so why wouldn't they?*

It is not uncommon for anyone who feels as if they were not cared for, or loved, or heard, growing up, to have holes in their hearts where basic needs lay unmet. Many of these people seek to fill this emptiness with a variety of things: money, material things, popularity, physical beauty, alcohol, addictions, work, being the best at whatever they do, demanding to maintain control, you name it. If the person who works so hard to obtain any one of these things would realize how temporal they are, maybe they would stop wasting all their time. The only thing that can fill the holes in a person's heart where pain has dug deep down and embedded its ugly head is the love of Christ our Savior. Revelation 3:17, 18 paints a pretty clear picture. These people think they have everything because they are wealthy, but Christ tells them they have nothing of true value.

Have you ever felt like you had to prove you were worth something? Did you ever feel like you had to prove to everyone and anyone that you were good? _____

What kinds of things did you find yourself doing to prove yourself? _____

_____

Did you ever accept the harsh treatment of someone just so that you would be getting some treatment rather than none at all?

_____

There is only one answer to this issue. Turn to John 13:23. How does the writer of this book, the disciple John, refer to himself in this passage? "The disciple whom _____."

John saw himself *first* as a person dearly loved by Jesus. I wonder, did Tamar have any idea that her Creator loved her and would one day send Jesus to us? When we live our lives without this foundational truth, we walk around trying to fill it with anything we can get our hands on. Some people may have taught us that love can be lost, that love is conditional, and that we do not matter. They may have tried to teach you that your worth lay in what you are able to do or in how you look. Maybe someone made you feel like you are not acceptable just the way you are? Or that your voice does not matter enough to be heard?

Turn to and read 1 John 4:13-19. Let this truth soak into the holes in your heart.

Fill in some blanks here: There is no _____ in love (v. 18). We know and _____ on the love _____ has for us (v. 16). We know God is always with us because He gave us His _____ (v. 13). We are able to love because God _____ loved _____ (v. 19).

One more thing: Who does Colossians 3:23, 24 say we work for? _____

. . . 🍃 . .

You are seen, heard, and loved by God. You matter, you are important, and you are good enough just the way you are. You can't lose God's love. My dear sister, I pray with all my heart that you may grow to see yourself FIRST not as an abused woman, but as a person Jesus loves. Find your significance in Him. Write out a prayer asking Him to help you remember that when you are feeling low. _____

_____

_____

_____

_____

_____

_____

_____

_____

_____

_____

Judgment

J udgment. (I feel like that word should come with some dramatic sound effects, something very *Star Wars*-worthy!) Have we not said things like, "So-and-so deserves it!" "When are they going to pay for what they did to so-and-so?" "How can God keep letting these things happen?" "I don't understand." You could probably add a few statements of your own, but the point is crystal-clear. We have to look at God's judgment before we move on. In Tamar's story, Absalom took judgment into his own hands. He felt that no one else on earth was going to do it, so he allowed the rage he felt toward the injustice done upon his sister to steal his entire life. We understand the point that when someone does something wrong, they should receive punishment for their crime. We have prisons packed full of that idea. We understand that we feel turmoil in our souls when people get away with heinous crimes. What I don't think we really understand, as a whole, is the incredible power of God's restraint. If we believe that God is the Creator, then we must believe that God is the destroyer that He says He is in His Word. Where we differ from God is in our desire to see His wrath now. We have limited vision and passionate hearts. God has world vision, without the restrictions of time, and a passionate heart.

Let's follow up with Absalom to complete Tamar's story. Allow me to recap the unfolding events for you. If you wish, you can read through chapter 19 to see how these events play out.

Absalom deviously plots to kill Amnon (2 Sam. 13). Absalom has a party, invites all the sons of the king, gets Amnon drunk, then has his men kill him (the first act in a long line of deception and cowardice). The rest of the brothers flee back to King David. Absalom flees to his grandfather's home for three years. David mourns terribly for Absalom (2 Sam. 13). David brings Absalom back to Jerusalem but refuses to see him for two years. Absalom is an attractive, well liked man. He has a family with three sons and a daughter, whom he names Tamar, after his sister (2 Sam. 14). Absalom plots to overthrow David with Amnon, the heir, out of the way. Absalom steals the hearts of the people of David's kingdom (2 Sam. 15:1-6). Absalom pretends to be honoring God as he sets the stage to overthrow David (2 Sam. 15:7-12). David flees from Absalom (2 Sam. 15:13-24). David accepts the consequences of his choices (2 Sam. 15:25, 26). Second Samuel 16 and 17 account the strife between father and son. In 2 Samuel 18, a battle rages between Absalom's army and David's army. Twenty-thousand-plus men die as a result (2 Sam. 18:7). David has ordered his men to protect Absalom, but they kill him instead (2 Sam. 18:9-17). David mourns for Absalom, returns to Jerusalem, and reclaims his throne (2 Sam. 18, 19).

Okay, wow. So Absalom's plotting did not go according to plan. Over twenty thousand men, men who were in the prime of their lives—brothers, fathers, sons, friends, husbands—perished for the mistakes of *three*. Do not let the magnitude of twenty thousand deaths pass over you too quickly. Allow the ripple effect of taking judgment into one's own hands become clear to you. We may wish to judge and order vengeance against a person who did us wrong, and surely twenty thousand men will not die as a result. The point to be taken here is that vengeance is not contained within the realm of the parties involved—everything we do touches other people's lives in one way or another. You may never know who is watching or how it affects them. This is one of the main reasons that God claims vengeance for Himself.

God is the only one capable to judge in all righteousness. Remember what Hebrews 4:12, 13 says? *Nothing* is hidden from God's sight. Not a single deed of a single man's heart. Not one motive for a single action is hidden from the Creator of the life it was born in. God also is the only one capable of seeing how one person's deeds will affect everything they come into contact with. God is also the only one who will truly know if that person's heart will turn to Him one day.

According to James 4:10-12, how many ultimate judges are there? _____

Why does He alone hold this authority? _____

_____

Read Matthew 10:26-28. Whom should we really fear? ____

_____

In this passage, Jesus tells us not to fear men who can only affect our living bodies. They cannot reach into our souls. They have no power over us in eternity, but God does.

This brings us to the second point: *God will judge*. God makes many promises in His Word. If we believe one, then we must believe them all. Ecclesiastes 11:9 reminds all to follow the ways of your heart, but to remember that God will bring you to judgment. We often ask God "why" questions like the ones at the beginning of today's lesson. These are understandable and I believe He listens to them, even if He does not always answer. But have you ever read an account of when God asks His people a "why" question? Turn to Ezekiel 33:11. God knows judgment will come upon the people, and He asks them, "Why! Why will you choose to die?" What a powerful perspective.

What else does this passage tell us about God's judgment? That He takes no _____ in the _____ of the _____. The only way a wicked person will ever change is when he turns to God. The acceptance and application of God's love and truth can do things inside a person no one would believe was possible. It can bring out the person God initially created them to be. Second Peter 3:9 explains that this desire is where God's patience comes from. He created man, He loves man; every man's soul is in God's hands. God must judge the earth in truth and righteousness. That means one day He will have to permanently separate Himself from His child. Go to and read Revelation 20:11-15. Whether or not we ever see God's judgment delivered on this earth, it will be done with finality in heaven.

There is a third point we would be foolish not to consider: *God's wrath is not pretty.* He goes to all lengths to save us from it because He loves us so very much. Hebrews 10:30, 31 assures us again of God's judgment and then notes that God's wrath is a dreadful thing to fall into. The Old Testament is really good at being vividly clear on these principles. Isaiah 66:15, 16 explains the execution of God's judgment upon all men. Deuteronomy 32:39-41 is pretty clear on this subject as well. Verse 41 highlights a very important thing for us to remember: Who does God say will feel His vengeance? Those who _____ Him. Those who turn from His ways in unrepentant wickedness. Those people who hurt you and then laugh about it. Those who try to manipulate you into believing you are the problem.

When we are wronged, we are tempted, sometimes, to the point of obsession (like Absalom), to take matters into our own hands. We have a driving need to see justice done now, although this is normally a one-sided affair—it is a rare occurrence for someone to request immediate judgment upon themselves. The truth of the matter is that no one is exempt from God's judgment unless they are covered by Christ. The inevitability of God's wrath should sharpen our focus on two more points today:

1. Trust that evil deeds will meet the Maker. Do not allow what has happened to you to take anything else from you. Your time on earth is a precious gift not to be wasted. Shift your focus from the need for someone to pay to the life God has waiting for you.

   Write out Romans 12: 21 to help you remember this. _____

   _____

   _____

2. Not only the people you consider evil will answer to God for their deeds. Someone you know and care for, even you yourself, will also stand before God's judgment. If they do

not know God, if they have not accepted the grace He offers to save them through Jesus, their fate will be worse than anything you can imagine. This thought should move you to the point of action. *You cannot be someone's savior,* but you can point them in the right direction. Often, all you may be able to do is pray for them. Sometimes, you simply need to live your life as an example of what God is able to do in a willing heart.

God requests this of you: Romans 12:18, 19. What does this request say? _____

_____

Let's close today with this thought: leave room for God to fulfill His own promises. Remember that love alone stays God's hand against us all, but only for a time. Based on what you learned today, have your thoughts on judgment been altered at all? If so, how? Do you care for someone who does not know the Lord? Does their ultimate fate stir anything inside you? _____

_____

_____

_____

_____

_____

_____

_____

_____

_____

_____

Week 4

Jesus, Peter, and Water Sports

God's Promise: God sees you for who you really are. You can do all things through Christ.

Do you believe this? _____

Why? Why not? _____

_____

_____

Satan's Lie: You are nothing. You can't turn from the past. No one even *wants* to see you.

Do you believe this? _____

Why? Why not? _____

_____

_____

It Is I

I am so thankful that you are still here. I know this work can be excruciating, but your healing is more than worth it. You are incredibly brave to go back and examine a place where no one wants to be. I am very proud of you; your courage will be rewarded. I am praying for you to rest in the peace Christ offers. I am praying for you to love and to feel loved with the heart God gave you. My sister, you are stronger than you think you are. And no matter what anyone has ever told you, you are good, you are loved, and you are not alone.

Today, we are going to look at God. Our goal is to see Him for who He really is. If you are sleepy, then go get some coffee, because we need focus today. There can be no Charlie Brown Wa-wa Wa-wa's this week! At every point of your healing, Satan will try to distract you and turn you from the truth. Do not allow him this victory! He knows that he is not stronger than God, but he relentlessly tries to best the LORD anyway. We humans are so easily distracted. Pray that God will sit with you as you complete today's lesson.

We are going to look at three different accounts of the same event. After walking with Jesus for a while, there came a point when the disciples had to see Him for who He really was in order to continue on as disciples. I also believe that Jesus came to a point where the disciples had to see Him for who He was in order for *Him* to continue on with *them*. To get a clear understanding of the situation we are about to encounter, we need to backtrack a little.

Turn to Matthew 14. The beginning of this chapter recounts the horrid death of John the Baptist. John was beheaded solely for the pleasure of Herod's lover's daughter. John had been imprisoned by Herod for speaking against his taking his brother's wife as a lover. This Herod is also the son of Herod the Great who had ordered all the baby boys in Bethlehem to be killed in an effort to eliminate the infant Jesus (Matt. 2:16). When Jesus heard the news of John's death, he was understandably very upset. Here, Jesus modeled the behavior we should follow when we are in situations that just don't make any sense to us: He went somewhere alone to pray (v. 13). Crowds of people followed Jesus. When He saw them, He set aside His own grief, had compassion on them, and blessed them (v. 14). The disciples saw that it was getting late, so they asked Jesus to send the people away to go find food for themselves. Jesus told the disciples to feed the crowd. The disciples kindly told Jesus that was impossible because they only had five loaves of bread and two fish (v. 15-17).

Pause here for a second. If you go back a few chapters, you will see that in chapter 10 Jesus gave the twelve disciples power and authority to perform miracles in His name (Matt. 10:1). Here, in this chapter, Christ is giving them an opportunity to have compassion on the people and to display the power He gave them. However, for whatever reason, the disciples were lacking in these areas. I believe Christ decided that drastic measures needed to be taken. After He fed all five-thousand-plus people, He found solitude once again to pray (v. 18-21). I can't help feeling tender towards Christ in this scene. The disciples had witnessed His miracles time and time again, yet they still displayed a lack of understanding about His love. I think they still just didn't get *who* Christ was. I think He was saddened not only by the recent, utterly horrid way a true believer had lost his life, but also at the thick-headedness of the twelve disciples.

The way in which Jesus gets these followers' attention is recorded by three different pens. Each author adds a specific detail about the event. When they are pieced together, we get a view of our Lord that is worth a little page-flipping. First read the account in Matthew 14:22-33.

What is Jesus doing in verse 23? _____

_____

Where had the boat carrying the disciples gone? _____

_____

Put your finger here for a second and take a peek at what Mark 6:48 adds to the event. The disciples were caught in the midst of a _____. (John 6:18 adds that the waters were rough.)

Back to Matthew 14:25, 26. Jesus decides that these guys need to finally understand who He is. He sees that the men are struggling against the rising storm, so He calmly steps onto the rough, windblown water. It is dark out, the disciples are distraught, and they mistake Jesus for a _____ (v. 26).

Take a look at Matthew 14:27, Mark 6:50, and John 6:20.

In every account Jesus is recorded saying: _____

_____

Something tells me that Jesus was not saying, "It is I, a man you are familiar with." I would have loved to have been able to witness the majesty and power of the voice that proclaimed, "IT IS I, the Messiah." Have you ever wanted someone to just look at you and see you for who you are? Because maybe if they can finally see into your heart they will understand you better? I believe this was the whole point.

Now Matthew's account injects a very good detail, for in it, we see that it is okay for us to ask God to strengthen our faith. Read verses 28 and 29. Peter needs a little boost in order to believe that Jesus is truly the Son of God out there in the storm, walking calmly on the water. Peter sees power that his human eyes do not understand. Often, God's might is too great for us to comprehend. Peter asks for proof, and Jesus grants his request. But, bless the dear man, he's about to get wet.

What happens in verse 30 when Peter stops looking at Jesus and focuses on the storm? _____

_____

_____

While Peter had his sight fixed on Jesus, he was able to walk on the water through the storm. When he allowed the storm to steal his focus, he began to fall. Do we not do the same when we allow our circumstances to take our eyes off of the one who can bring us through them? Sometimes I walk with Him on the water and sometimes I get really wet. But, thankfully, He never leaves me in the ocean alone. He is always there, like Jesus was for Peter, with an outstretched hand and a reminder of faith.

What happens in verse 31? _____

_____

Verse 32 tells us that when Jesus climbed in the boat, the wind died down.

Now flip back over to John 6:21, because in it we see another very interesting point. What does this piece of the event say? _____

_____

_____

After they saw Jesus for who He really was, they were *willing* to take Him into the boat. I think the disciples had to be willing to accept that Jesus was the Messiah before Jesus could teach them anything else. We can only go so far in our walk with God until we acknowledge who God is. Is God a warm and fuzzy idea, or is He real? Was Jesus just a good man, or was He the Son of God? Believing the unexplainable takes faith, and as soon as faith was decided on, the boat got where it was going (v. 21).

Now, one more very important tidbit that Mark 6:51, 52 provides.

Why had the disciples not understood what Jesus was trying to teach them with the whole crowd-and-bread ordeal? _____

_____

For whatever reason, those men had not taken that final, defining leap of faith. Their doubts or their unbelief, however you wish to label it, hardened their hearts. There were twelve men. I am sure you can have a wide variety of issues with twelve people. Sometimes, when I attend a Bible study at my church that runs an average of one hundred ladies (or so) per semester, my heart is acutely aware of the scope of issues in the room. Each person weathers their own storms in their own little boats. Some of them have their Savior with them, and some of them are still straining against a wind much too powerful for their arms. Once the disciples knew Jesus was the Christ, they were amazed and they worshiped Him. They had walked with Him, heard His teaching, and seen His miracles. But it was not until this point, when Christ walked steadily through adversity, that they knew for sure who their friend really was.

When you are up against something too big for you, the only way you won't drown is to put God between you and the person, issue, or situation. Jesus taught the disciples that if they could see Him for who He really was, nothing would ever separate them from Him. There is no abuse too horrendous. No soul too lost. No sister too scared or too scarred. No sin too great. No person too challenging to deal with. Nothing. When you focus on God, the problem you are facing is much less daunting. When you maintain eye contact, it is easier to keep your faith strong. It is also easier to hear whatever He may be directing you to do. If you don't have much faith, ask for more. It's okay to do that.

How strong do you feel your faith is?_____

_____

_____

_____

Does your faith seem to strengthen or weaken when you are dealing with something really hard? How can you tell? _____

_____

_____

_____

_____

What do you normally do when you feel a storm a-comin'? ____

_____

_____

If you know deep inside that Jesus is who He says He is, what brought you to that realization? _____

_____

_____

_____

_____

If you don't know yet, do not be troubled. That may be one reason why you are doing this study. Pray for God to help you with this doubt. He will. _____

_____

_____

_____

_____

_____

Can you think of just one situation that God may be asking for you to focus on Him and allow Him to calm the waters? _____

_____

_____

_____

_____

_____

God of the House of God

Today, we are continuing our mission to see God for who He really is. When we begin to understand that fact, as we learned yesterday, our faith is strengthened. We are going to dig into another account of Jesus showing Himself to the disciples in order to accomplish that very thing. Today's events differ in that the disciples had lost Jesus to a physical death and they did not know where to turn. Life had left them in a place where they no longer knew what was up or down. They sat between the terrible Friday and the glorious Sunday. I know that you know what I mean: that moment after the tragedy, but before the moving on. The "What in the world am I supposed to do now?" stage. At some point in time, anyone who walks the earth will know the lost feeling these kinds of days hold.

Turn with me to John 21. Read verses 1-14, and let's break them down.

Verses 1, 2: The disciples were trying to figure out how to live their day-to-day lives without their anchor. Jesus had been crucified. Many of them had turned from Him. They were deep in sorrow and at a loss for what to do next. They had seen Jesus twice after He rose, but they had not yet received the Great Commission, which gave their lives clear direction from Jesus (Matt. 28:18-20). They also had not yet been filled with the Holy Spirit, which Jesus said would be their guidance (John 14:16).

Verse 3: Peter has a bright idea to revert back to his old ways. He was a fisherman when Jesus found him. He knew that way of life, so he went back to it (Matt. 4:18, 19). This is an all-too-common plan of attack. Fishing is innocent enough, but some of us have had slightly shadier habits. Do not make the mistake of thinking that the lady who sits next to you on the church pew may never have battled with addictions, promiscuity, selfishness, pride, anger, loss, guilt, or pain. Chances are, if you got her alone and she opened up to you, your eyes would be forced to see that we come from all walks of life. What makes her look like she might not have known trouble in her life is the love of her Savior that she wraps around herself like a shield. Anyone worth knowing has fallen down at least once.

Do you ever remember going back to your old way of doing things when times got a little hot? _____

_____

How did that work out for you? Did you make many mistakes?

_____

_____

Verse 3: Everyone else thought that was a grand idea, so they stayed out all night long fishing. But their nets remained empty.

Verse 4: Jesus was there, but they could not recognize Him. They were still trying to make things work their own way. Jesus waited patiently for someone to look up and take notice of Him.

Verse 5: Jesus calls out to them. Figuratively speaking, He knocks on their doors. I love this part. Sometimes I am certain that God has a great sense of humor. Jesus says, "Hey fellas, how are y'all doing out there?" (As you can see, my Jesus is from Texas!) (Just kidding.)

How do the disciples have to answer? _____

_____

I hope you wrote "truthfully." When God asks us a question, it would be best just to answer in all honesty. (I remember always answering questions in conversations or in Bible studies with what I thought was the right answer. I wanted to look and feel like I had things covered, but all I was accomplishing was prolonging the chance of any real growth. There is such peace and freedom in being able to say you don't have all the right answers.) The disciples were not doing well without Jesus. Their long night of work hadn't reaped any rewards. I never got anywhere trying to do things without God, either. Usually, things just got even more difficult on my own, more confusing. The answers I professed having in public evaporated in private, the disconnect between heart and head blatantly apparent.

Verse 6: Jesus gives them an abundant miracle, and as they are pulling in their haul, they still do not see that Jesus is the one who provided it. So far, no one really looked to see who it came from. Note that they did muster the last ounce of strength they had to obey Jesus's direction and they caught a ton of fish. They may have been doubtful and not quite sure of what to expect, but they did follow. This bit of Scripture also shows a depth of kindness from our Lord. In it, we see that when Jesus was trying to get the disciples' attention, He chose to provide them with a miracle that would potentially remind them of their time with Him. He gave them something to resonate in their souls. Have you ever had that kind of feeling? Something deep and thick, solid and unexplainable? Something that could not be explained as a coincidence?

_____

_____

_____

Verse 7: The disciple who *knew* Jesus loved him was the first to recognize that Christ was there with them. Think about that a second.

Is it not true that when you really feel loved by someone, it is easier to have a relationship with them? The more confident you are of God's love for you, the easier it will be for you to see how He is working in your life. The more you know He loves you, the more you will be able to see Him around you.

Was there ever a time when you *know* you "saw" God? A time when you heard His direction clearly, saw His work being done, or felt His presence? _____

_____

Verses 7, 8: They are so excited! Peter jumps overboard to get to Jesus! The rest follow in the boat.

Verse 9: When they get to shore, they see that Jesus already has a fire going. He has already begun to cook some fish that *did not* come from their catch.

I think this symbolizes that when we follow God's directions and we go to Him, He has more blessings for us than we even know about. It's like God is saying, "I have so much more that I want to give you, if you will just look to Me. Trust Me, follow My direction, and you won't even be able to count your blessings." Please, please tune out that voice that is saying you have done too much wrong to have God's blessing, if you are hearing that right now. God is so forgiving! True repentance opens the door to God's lasting blessings.

Look up Ephesians 3:14-21 and allow this message to soak into your mind and heart. You get strength from faith. You get faith from Christ, and Christ can do more than you could ever imagine.

What are we strengthened through? _____

_____

Can the power of God's love be defined within the bounds of human reason? _____

Verse 10: Jesus brings up a good point here: When you come to God, remember what He has done for you. Jesus says, "Bring to me what I have given you." Remembering what God has done in your life or in the lives of people you know can greatly strengthen your faith. As a matter of fact, I think God requires us to keep in mind the things He has done. They are testimonies to His power and glory. Say, for instance, you have learned a second language. You now have the ability to speak to others who understand that language. If you don't ever use it, over time, it will weaken. Eventually, it will be forgotten; faith is not so different.

Verse 11: Peter has already jumped ship, so he had to go back and get his fish. How very like Peter! How like all of us at times. It is easy to forget our dependence on God when things are going well, isn't it?

Verse 12-14: Jesus serves them again. The Master serves the people. He is never so controlling that He *must* sit on His throne and be served at all cost—that lesser people *must* bow and scrape beneath Him—though He holds every right to that position. He has not come to teach us to be kings. He has come to teach us to love. The funny thing is that when we truly encounter the love of Christ, we can't stop bowing down to Him. This kind of worship comes from being touched by that love that surpasses knowledge and being granted a choice to embrace it.

You are traveling along a difficult journey. You will need strength and clarity. You are going to hit rough patches and you will need guidance through them. When you are in these situations, do not just look at the things of God. Don't only focus on miracles you have seen or heard about. Do not think that just attending church or Sunday school is going to fix things. Please do not pray repetitious prayers that you could say in your sleep in two seconds flat. Look to *the God* of the House of God. Seek to connect with *Him*.

Take a quick look at an old friend. Jacob turned into Israel after he encountered God. We will get into that amazing lesson another day, but today look at the particular way in which Jacob's focus shifted from the things of God to God Himself. This only happened after a terrible tragedy within Jacob's family occurred. Distraught, Jacob prayed to God, and was told to go back to the place he first met his Lord. (Enter remembering what God had done in his life.)

Back in Genesis 28:10-19, God confirmed the covenant He made with Abraham to Jacob. Jacob had a dream and realized that God was there. When Jacob woke up, he built an altar and named the place Bethel. "Bethel" means "House of God." Jacob had seen the *things of God* in his dream.

Read Genesis 35:1-7, which recounts Jacob's shifting focus. One important aspect of this story is that Jacob has his entire household get rid of their old ways completely (v. 2-4). The idols that his people worshiped distracted Jacob from moving forward in his faith. Jacob turned from his old ways and placed them as far out of sight as possible. Then, and only then, was Jacob able to focus on God.

When he gets back to Bethel, Jacob has realized that he has been focusing on the wrong things. Jacob renames the place where he first encountered God "El-Bethel," which means "God of the House of God."

Do you have anything that represents God to you? Your church, music, house decorations, jewelry, books, whatever you think about when you think about God? _____

_____

Do you take comfort in having these things? Why? _____

_____

Would they mean anything at all to you if God were not connected to them in some way? _____

_____

Having mementos is not wrong. They can give you great comfort. Focusing on the "things," instead of the God who makes them special, is where the problem lies. The entire point today is to realize that God is always there waiting for you to look at *Him*. He can help. He will help. He wants to bless you above anything you could have imagined. He wants, above all else in this world, for you to believe that He is who He says He is. Each person connects with God in a unique way. Maybe that is why God gave Himself so many different names in the Bible: God the Healer, God the Redeemer, God the Father, God the Provider. If you really want to get a taste of that business, complete a Bible study on the names of God. He even allowed cast-out slave girls in their distress and worship to give Him a name.

What name does Hagar give to God in Genesis 16:13? (Don't skip this one.)

The God who _____.

Our God is the God who sees us. Down to bare bones and clear through our hearts. Is there anything that you are hoping God does not see? Be brave and uncover it, for He sees it anyway. Go ahead and set aside any fear of judgment or shame. You will not be ridiculed when you go to God in truth. He can see you as you are. Now it is time for us to see Him as He is.

Take some time today in the still quiet of your heart to ask God to help you see Him. Don't get up too quickly. Lay your distractions down, close your eyes, and open your spirit to Him.

Lord, vividly, gently, meet with us here, I pray.

What Does God Want from You?

I don't know about you, but there came a time in my walk with God that I needed to know what He was asking from me. Have you ever asked, "Lord, what do You want from me?" I do believe the answer to this question changes with our growth and circumstances. We may come to a point where we are capable of doing things that we had not yet been able to accomplish. Five years ago, I could not have typed a single day of this study.

Is there anything that you really want to do, but for some reason are not able to do? Be specific. Think, "No limits." _____

_____

_____

Why can't you do this? _____

_____

Maybe we lack the confidence or the knowledge to accomplish these dreams. Of course, there are some things that we can wish to do that realistically may never happen. I seriously doubt that I will ever become an Olympic High Dive Gold Medalist. But, friend, let me tell you, every time I jump off that little diving board at the local pool, my mind takes me there. I have neither the knowledge nor the physical ability. Thankfully, the lifeguards do not require me to be professionally proficient at diving before they allow me to step on the board. I do, however, have to know enough about swimming not to drown.

This is one reason why I believe that there are a few specific basics God is asking of all His children.

Turn with me (I say that a bunch, don't I?) to Micah 6:8.

What does this verse say God is asking of you? _____

_____

_____

Do the right thing first. Remember the mercy He has shown you and pass it on. Walk humbly with Him. Three very basic statements. Sometimes they are easier said than done, but each is a necessity. I am drawn to this last requirement because it is foundational. When you walk beside someone, you can hear what they say to you. You can see them clearly. You appear to be on some form of level ground when you walk beside a person. We would be foolish to ever assume that we are in any way equal with God. Pride causes many feet to stumble along that path. For this reason, the word "humbly" is included in the passage. God's love for us is so profound that He will allow us to walk beside Him. There are definitely times that God goes before us to clear an obstacle from our path. He does this in order to make a way for His will to be done. But time and time again, He lowers Himself to an attainable status for His creation. He never lessens His authority, He simply increases His availability.

How many security personnel would separate you from, say, taking a morning stroll with your favorite celebrity? _____

_____

They would have to invite you and inform the security detail just to allow you into their space. In Micah 6:8, we have an open invitation to walk with God every single day. We don't have to have any clout or any special status. We are special enough solely because we are His.

We should look at another request God makes of His children. Open your Bible to Mark 9:14-29.

What has happened in this scene? _____

_____

Why do you think the disciples could not heal the boy when his father begged them to? _____

_____

Check out an interesting fact in verse 14. What were the teachers of the law doing with the disciples while they were trying to heal the boy? _____

_____

Also, glance back through the first section of chapter 9. Jesus had chosen just three of the disciples to witness His transfiguration on the mountain. Do you think the other disciples may have been feeling a bit put out? Or less important? _____

_____

How well do you handle situations when you are feeling stressed, or hurt, or left out? _____

_____

When we look closely at the demon-possessed boy's father, we see one major reason for the record of this account. The boy's father begs Jesus to help him. He says, "If you can do anything, help us." So far, to this man, Jesus holds the same status as His disciples. They were not able to heal the boy, so he was not sure if Jesus could either. Jesus answers him in verse 23 with what declaration?

_____

_____

On a side note, this scene should help us remember that when we display a lack of faith, it can affect a stranger. Not to sound creepy, but we live in a crowded world; there is always someone watching. The key to what Jesus meant, exactly, by this statement lies in verse 29, but we must look at the father's response first. What does the boy's father ask Jesus to increase? _____

_____

Here again we see that it is okay to express your doubts to God. He will increase your faith if you ask Him to. Jesus greatly increased this man's faith when He healed his son. If you flip over to Matthew 17:21, which retells the same account, you will see that Jesus tells the disciples only *true faith* the size of a mustard seed is required to accomplish the impossible. Isn't it comforting to know that God does not require us to be ten feet tall and bulletproof? He only requires us to have faith as tiny as a seed. Have you ever actually held a mustard seed in the palm of your hand? Here, let me give you an idea of how big it is: * There, that little asterisk is the same size as the amount of faith required from God. I think the point is that the faith is there, real, not assumed or imagined. He says to give Him that much, then stand back and watch. Hear Him crack His knuckles; see Him move some mountains.

Take a pause here in the story to hear from a sister whose path was changed by a Savior who said, "It's okay to ask for help, no matter where you find yourself." I will honestly say that I was so judgmental for a long time towards women who made some really poor choices. (Ahem, let me get this plank out of my eye so I can continue typing.) I arrogantly dismissed the fact that pain, confusion, and exhaustion can weaken even the most steadfast spirit, not to mention what they can do to someone just trying to survive. I can't share all of her story with you, but I will say that she met her Savior in the midst of her sin, He believed her to be worth His time, and she accepted His grace. (At least she knew she needed it!)

> *Every time before it happened, I would tell myself, "I'm NOT going to make this choice." The moment would come, I would fall, and I would be immersed in the lie of temporal satisfaction. I would black out every aspect of life around me and focus only on the thing of the moment. The thing that made me feel less empty for about a second. I would leave the situation in a state of confusion and then the guilt would set in. The shame of my actions would make me want to die. After a while I didn't even know who I was anymore. I was a physical and emotional wreck. I was behaving in a way that was so far removed from the person I am that I didn't even recognize myself. I knew I was a child of God. Why wouldn't He just TAKE it from me?! I didn't want to be the person I was being at all.*
>
> *One evening, on my knees, on my bedroom floor, through my guilty, shameful tears, I prayed for the hundredth time for these choices to end. But something was different this time. Instead of asking God to take this thing from me, I prayed that He would help me make different choices. I began to think that maybe He*

*wasn't intervening because there was some action required on my part. The word "obedience" kept floating through my mind. I knew I could not be obedient on my own, so I asked for help. What happened next caught me so off guard that it altered my entire outlook. I swear I heard Jesus say, "**I will pray for you.**"*

I was shaken to my core. WHY would Jesus pray for me?! I was making choices that were directly against His teaching and I KNEW BETTER. It wasn't like I had never been taught right from wrong. I was spitting in the Bible's face every time I fell to that !@#$% addiction! Even still, Jesus was with me in that room, on that floor, listening to my prayers, and He said "I will pray for you." It seems He knew I was not capable of turning my life around without a little help. It seems He still thought I was worth the intervention of His intercessory prayers. Was He just waiting for me to say "Please help me choose differently" instead of "Please just take this away"?

*Looking back on this time in my life, I think that my faith, more than my heartache and confusion, was the real issue. Life was hard, and I don't think I believed it would ever be any different, so it makes sense that I fell to temporal distractions. I believed in God, but I didn't have much faith that He would ever fulfill my needs. Faith is an anchor that can't be manufactured. Mine didn't truly begin to grow until Jesus sat on that floor with me. I think He was telling me that now that I was **really** ready to try, He was going to help.*

Go back to Mark 9:22, where the father asks Jesus if He can help. Do you think maybe the disciples were waiting with bated breath to see what was going to happen next? _____

_____

They were Jesus's disciples and they had not been able to heal the boy. Was there maybe something bigger going on, or did they just allow the taunting of the lawmakers to weaken their faith with distractions? When they are alone with Jesus, they ask Him why they failed. The answer Jesus gives them is best written in the King James Version. Verse 29 states: "This kind can come forth by nothing, but by prayer and fasting."

Why do you think prayer is necessary to overcome an impossible situation? _____

_____

What do you think fasting added to the mix that prayer alone did not cover? _____

_____

Fasting as a religious practice is designed to direct complete focus on God and what He has called you to do during the time of the fast. Jesus was showing the disciples that they were facing a serious issue, one that took a deeper level of attention on, and belief in, God's abilities. Prayer is essential because it is the way we communicate with God. Fasting was necessary in this situation because complete focus on God alone was needed to overcome the problem they were faced with. Everything else needed to be blocked out. Nothing could be allowed to distract their attention from the request they were laying at God's feet. The disciples had allowed the lawmakers, the crowd, and their insecurities to distract them. That is why they could not free the boy.

What tends to distract you from your prayers? _____

_____

When you wonder what God wants from you, remember these three things: (1) Walk with Him so that you may know Him better. (2) Have faith in Him. (3) Ask for more faith when you need it.

What a wonderful thing it would be to see God turn this *into this*. That, right there, would be some mighty faith. We may only receive that amount in heaven, but who knows? Have you asked Him?

Close today by remembering that God does not expect you to be without flaw. He knows how human we are. He knows we will never be perfect here. But He will always love you and be here to help you when you ask. Do you want to ask for help in any specific situation today? _____

_____

God Sees You Exactly as Who He Made You to Be

Even when we do not feel like we have anything to offer or anything good inside us, God's vision is still able to cut to the very essence of our beings. One of the most heartbreaking things to witness is a woman who cannot see that she is worth anything. When children are young, they must be made to feel like they are loved, special, good, beautiful no matter what, intelligent, capable, cared for, listened to. They *must* feel like they matter. When a person does not feel like they matter or that they are seen, it is extremely difficult for them to view themselves correctly. They begin to take others' visions as their own. Many times, those other people have sight far more limited than the child's, for they are only willing to see their selfish desires. This can then manifest into a driving need for someone to think highly of said child. He or she may take drastic measures in order to get people to like them and treat them as worthy. Most of the time, this only inflicts further damage on an already wounded child.

Did anyone, or any circumstance you were in, ever tell you that you held little worth? What? Who? _____

_____

_____

Did you believe them? Why? _____

_____

How did that situation change the way you viewed yourself? Did you do things with peers or at school to try to fit in, be accepted, be liked? _____

_____

Do you feel that your past is a taint covering the person you wish to be? _____

_____

When this study is complete, I am going to ask you questions about cute little puppy dogs and what your favorite movie or book is, but right now we have work to do. I know these questions are difficult, but in order to deal with the issues, they must be brought to the surface. Dig deep, pray for strength, and lay it all out there so that God can speak truth into your life.

Today, we are going to look at a person who actually felt like he was nothing. His family had been living under attack from other people for seven years. They had also been living with their backs turned to God. We will meet a scared young man and God will show us a mighty warrior. Turn to Judges 6 and read the first half of this chapter, stopping at verse 24.

Why were the Israelites living in such a state of turmoil? (v .9, 10) _____

_____

Because of his family's actions, and those of the tribe, Gideon is found living in hiding with a constant threat shadowing his life. We meet him here attempting to salvage any food possible by hiding it from the enemies who continually overpower his people and steal their provisions. God takes a seat under the shade of an oak to speak with Gideon. These verses imply that God was watching Gideon for a bit before He revealed Himself to the young man. He seems to be waiting for Gideon to notice Him. It can be very hard to see anything aside from the struggle we face, so God calls out to Gideon.

What is the first thing God says to Gideon? (v. 12) _____

_____

"O mighty man of valor," as the King James Version reads, or "mighty warrior" in the NIV. Is it comforting to see that no matter what has happened in your life, the core, the spirit, of what God created inside you has not been altered? You may think it has been, but it hasn't. One time, someone asked me why I had finally set my mind on healing, and for once the answer came easily to me. I said "I just wanted to *know* her, that woman God created in me, as she would have been if she hadn't been raped."

However you want to say it, God sees far more in Gideon than Gideon sees in himself. What is Gideon's response to God in verse 13?

_____

_____

Try to visualize this scene. What kind of expression is Gideon wearing? What do you think is going through his mind? What would be the first thought in your head if someone walked right up to you and called you a mighty-anything-*good*? _____

_____

Gideon asks the first thing that most people who feel abandoned ask: "Where has God been?" "Where were His miracles when we needed them?" "We have all heard of His wonder." This is understandable, coming from someone living a desperate life. Remember that Gideon grew up in a family who had turned from God, though. At this point, Gideon does not realize he has encountered God. Glance back at verse 10. What does the very last sentence say? _____

The generations that preceded Gideon had chosen not to follow God, and now Gideon was dealing with the repercussion of their sins. I know many of you who come from childhood abuse can relate. Even if the abuse did not come from a parent or family member, the person who abused you could have been living in generational sin. We are going to talk more about that tomorrow.

Above all that Gideon can see and knows, God breathes life into him with this encounter. Maybe God was just waiting for someone from this tribe to listen to Him. We know from His Word that He wishes for all men to turn to Him. He does not want to lose even one of His children. We also know that the choice of that matter rests solely on the individual to see God and listen when He calls. Even so, Gideon needed a little help. God relentlessly pursues His children. This passage teaches us that when God looks at us, He can see the person He created us to be beneath all that could ever bury us. Gideon was allowed to vent the frustrations and questions of his heart. Then, God looked deep inside Gideon, and said, "Go in the strength you have, and save Israel out of Midian's hand. Am I not sending you?" (v. 14)

Try to take in the magnitude of what Gideon is hearing. He is being charged to turn from everything he knows and save his family. He's being asked to stand up against foes that have continually threatened and harmed his family. Really, what he is being asked to do is face a giant, and he is feeling a bit too small for that.

Parents can think of this as being told to turn from their old habits to save their children's future. Many people can look at this as a call to be different from all that you have ever known. Set out to make a better life for yourself and anyone who depends on you. Does anyone depend on you? Who? _____

_____

Notice that God specifically states that He has *created in* Gideon the strength to carry this request out.

Gideon feels useless; he sees insurmountable odds against him. God listens while Gideon runs down a list of reasons why he is so *not* a mighty warrior, thank you very much, in verse 15. How does God answer Gideon's fear in verse 16? _____

_____

When God asks us to be mightier than we believe ourselves to be, He always reminds us that He is with us. We go into battle with the power of the mightiest Warrior of all. We NEVER go alone. God knows that there are things we cannot face without His help.

Even still, Gideon needed a sign (or two, or three) from God that he was hearing things correctly. We see here once again that it is okay to ask God to help you with your doubt. Gideon brought an offering to the Lord, and God accepted it. Sometimes we have very little to bring as an offering. That makes no matter whatsoever; just bring what you have. If all you have at the moment is doubt, anger, fear, issues upon issues—bring them to Him. If all you have is a broken body and sleepless nights, lay them at His feet. What if you have addictions, people you can't deal with, emptiness in your heart, cold in your bones? Bring it all. The point is that you *bring it* and meet with God, so that God can heal you. He will turn your tears into treasures.

After God accepts Gideon's offering, He vanishes from Gideon's sight (v. 21). Take special note in the next part of this account. Though Gideon could no longer see with his eyes the angel of the Lord, was God still with him? (v. 23) _____ YES! And, even better yet, what did God rest upon Gideon in this same verse? ____ _____ That Gideon *felt* the peace and *knew* it came from God is confirmed in verse 24 when he declares that: _____ _____. Peace like that is more than the refreshment of a deep, steady breath; it is unexplainable calm and solidity.

We have seen some deep truth today. A little recapping would be wise; I do not want you to miss a single point.

1. God can look past everything that we have ever done or that has happened to us and see the true, unique qualities He created in us. We are God's workmanship. Write out Ephesians 2:10: _____

    _____

    _____

YOU are God's workmanship. God prepared amazing things in advance for you. Do you want to know what life with your Savior is like? As I write this, I pray for you, individually—each and every hand that this study will be placed into. I laugh every single day from the joy in my soul that God has given me. There were months upon months, years upon years, as a child, when I did not even smile.

2. Peace through any situation only comes from God. It also only comes when we trust God and continually focus on Him. Write out Isaiah 26:3: _____

_____

"Steadfast" is defined as "fixed or unchanging; steady; firmly loyal or constant." "Steadfast" means "unswerving." God is the only thing that never changes. The love of God never alters its attributes. It remains unconditional, unswerving, loyal to each and every heart that allows it to rest upon it. Do you know someone whose love is conditional, someone who only shows you love when you toe their very specifically drawn lines? Do you worry about losing it—and them? This is not a concern you will bear with your Savior. Make no mistake: God does draw specific lines for our protection, but the difference is He never snatches His love away from us when we step out of bounds.

3. Though we will not feel God's presence or clearly see His work our every waking moment, He is with us always. Just like when the angel of the Lord vanished from Gideon's sight—God was still there. After Gideon met God face-to-face, Gideon could hear Him without directly laying eyes on Him. We do not walk away from a meeting with the Lord unchanged.

What is in your heart at this very moment? _____

_____

_____

How do you honestly see yourself? _____

_____

_____

Pray that God will reveal to you how He sees you. _____

_____

_____

Generational Sin

Yesterday we saw how Gideon's life was affected by his father's sins. Today, we will attempt to lay to rest the issue of generational sin. How do you feel about this topic? Does it make you uncomfortable? Does it make you angry? Does it make you feel defeated? _____

_____

_____

I will be honest with you: before I studied this topic, I hated it. I did not understand the principles of what God teaches His people in this. I thought that my father's and mother's sin was somehow going to condemn me for the rest of my life, no matter my choices about how I would live. Did I not have a choice in the matter?! Would the choices that I made overshadow my children all their days? I did the only thing a girl can do when something does not sit right: I went in search of answers.

It may be helpful to take a bit of an elementary approach to this topic. Please do not allow familiarity of a Scripture to cause you to skim over any of these points. Each time you study God's Word, you are given an opportunity to discover a deeper, or completely new, truth.

1. **Sin and confusion enter the world.** Turn to and read Genesis 3:1-7.

Satan is described here as a _____ snake (v. 1). He comes to Eve and poses a question to her. Notice how first she answers him with what God has told her and Adam (v. 2, 3). Then, Satan manipulates what has been said. He tells Eve, "You _____ shall not _____!" (v. 4) Satan alludes only to a physical death, although he knows very well that God means a spiritual death caused by separation from Him brought on by sin. Satan tells a half-truth to Eve. He banks on the fact that only a piece of the truth will be strong enough to sway her judgment. This is the first time we ever see the immediate desires of man eclipse the repercussions of disobedience. While man sought God first, he walked continually with Him in paradise. When man chose to do things according to a selfish desire, the world as we know it was created. Instant gratification speaks to *self* alone. Sadly, the ripple effect of the sin a person commits is great.

Now read Genesis 3:8-24.

Verse 8 is an extremely powerful bit of Scripture when we look closely at it. Adam and Eve, having passed the *momentary* enjoyment of their apple, now must face the truth. They hear God coming and they hide from Him. Why did they hide if they did not know that they had done wrong? The tree of life had given man the ability to see both good and bad. When God creates a person, He creates them *good* with the *ability to choose between good and bad.* Once Adam and Eve chose "bad," He had to allow them the consequences of their actions. In verse 9, God says to them, "Show yourselves to Me." I feel like this tells us that at some point in time, we will face the choices we make, and answer to the One who made us. The rest of this chapter, which is too deep to tread lightly upon in a short study, explains the consequences of their actions. All the earth, man, beast, and land bore those consequences. We lost the *continual physical presence* of God with us on the earth. We will only get that back in heaven.

2. **Sin crouching at every door.** Read the first time sin is mentioned by name in the Word in Genesis 4:7. What does this passage imply about the nature of sin? _____

This passage appears to be saying that Satan is reaching for anyone who may teeter on the edge of a choice. When faced with a situation where we have to make a choice, or face a wrong that has been done, by either ourselves or another, we can overcome sin by being mature enough to seek the truth. That means admitting that judgment belongs to God. That means taking responsibility for your own actions. It also means getting to the place where you take a step back, evaluate the situation, and then ask God what should be done. When this is done, instead of acting rashly in emotion, when we respond to a situation instead of reacting, we are slamming the door in Satan's face. It is very difficult to turn the other cheek. It is even more difficult to accept criticism or admit a wrong. But when you don't, sin is no longer crouching at your door, he is devouring you.

3. **Creation of life.** First read Psalm 51:5. What are your thoughts on this verse? _____

_____

The NIV reads, "Surely I was sinful at birth, sinful from the time my mother conceived me." The King James Version and the New American Standard both read, "Behold I was [shapen / brought forth] in iniquity, and in sin did my mother conceive me." To me, these translations seem to read very differently, so I went in search of the original language definitions. The word *iniquity* here in Hebrew is *avon*, which means "perversity, moral evil." The word for *sin* in this verse is "chet," meaning a crime or its penalty. This word comes from the root word "chata" which means "to miss, to sin, to forfeit, lack, expiate, repent, lead astray, condemn."

When the meaning of these words is understood, they lead us to a very simple truth: We are born into a sinful world. The sin in this world will leave no one unscathed. If we read that God created man "good" and gave him the free gift to choose between good and bad, how, then, can we ever think that God creates a soul bad? This is such a tender subject when opened in the light of rape victims who become pregnant. Have you ever felt that a resulting child from rape will be bad simply because of the father's actions? Please be

honest; there is no judgment here. _____
_____ If you have a child that came to
you in this way, look at them as a child of God, for that is what
they are. God allowed that life to be conceived because HE is their
maker and HE has plans for them. If you had an abortion because
of rape, PLEASE complete a Bible study on forgiveness. When you
accepted Christ as your Savior, a new creation was awakened in you.
You have already been forgiven for this deed. You need to know
it so that you may walk with your God. If you have never had an
abortion, PLEASE do not be a stumbling block for those women
who are trying to put their lives back together. If either one of these
topics concern you, write in your journal all that is inside you about
it and bring it to group. The women leading this study are here to
extend the love and acceptance of God to you. Be brave. Turn from
the lies of Satan that try to confuse you even more.

4. **Saving Grace.** Exodus 20:4-6, at first glance, sounds very
harsh and unfair. This Scripture clearly states that the
iniquities of the father will be passed down to the children
four generations. This is the Scripture I had a real problem
with until I noticed what it really says. Write out verse 6: __

_____

_____

_____

That one little word *but* is saving grace because it is a promise
to anyone who will turn to God. The sins of their fathers hold no
sway over them any longer. God is saying if you choose to live with
your back to Me, then you will live with the repercussions of the
sin you live in. BUT, if you turn to God, you will not be punished.
God may allow you to reap what you sow for the poor choices you
make, but remember what Romans 6:23 says—"For the wages of
sin is death"—and we who accept Christ's gift of redemption get to
reap the second half of Romans 6:23, which says, _____

_____

_____.

5. **Learning right from wrong.** God clearly states throughout Scripture that parents must teach their children right from wrong. Deuteronomy 6:4-9 gives one example of the importance God places on teaching children about the Lord's ways. Proverbs 22:6 tells parents to _____

_____

_____ This verse from Proverbs even allows for the uniqueness of all children to be cherished. No two children are the same. They all need to be treated as individual people, who express emotions differently, have different needs and interests, and should be taught accordingly. Where one child may need more firm discipline, another may learn from a warning. The point is, God shows us that children are all different, but they all need guidance.

When a child grows up in an environment where their parent's or parents' lives are full of sin, what does that child learn? If all they are taught is to lie, cheat, steal, and be selfish, chances are that when they are grown, they will follow this path. *This* is generational sin: sin learned from watching caregivers live sinful lives. Sin learned from an environment of no boundaries where children are exposed to anything and everything. When a person reaches an age where they are able to make their own choices, they can either continue on in that sin or attempt to learn a different way of life. Our old friend Gideon went in the strength God gave him and turned from that life. For a time, he chose to walk with God. We are all given this choice.

Do you feel you have a choice about the way you live your life? Why? Why not? _____

_____

_____

_____

Lord, help us see that with You, we can overcome *anything*, I pray, Amen.

Week 5

Betrayal and Boundaries

God's Promise: God will never leave or stop loving you. Your voice is and should be heard. You can trust again. You don't have to be afraid.

Do you believe this? _____

Why? Why not? _____

_____

_____

Satan's Lie: No one loves you. You can't trust anyone. You don't matter. Everyone will leave you when they get to know who you **really** are.

Do you believe this? _____

Why? Why not? _____

_____

_____

But It Was YOU!

Oh the lies that we believe in this area. I have been looking forward to discussing this week's lesson with you my sister. I know how difficult life is when we sit here. How betrayal and pain can affect just about everything we do. How we can generalize what one person has done to us over the entire human race. A lot of the time we don't even realize that we may be doing it. Check off the things you might have caught yourself thinking from time to time:

- What is that person thinking about me? They look mad; what did I do?
- Those women are whispering together. What are they saying about me? I know they are!
- I look awful today, everyone is staring at me!
- He is looking at me strangely. How does he know what happened to me?!
- So-and-so never loved me; *he* sure as heck won't. Not *really* love me.
- I could not trust so-and-so; I can't trust anyone.
- Those girls in school never liked me. I'll never have any real friends ...

You get the picture. These thoughts come from insecurity born of pain, betrayal, and lack of boundaries.

Betrayal. That is a four-letter word if I have ever heard one. In all honesty, betrayal can be given just as easily as it is received. We have to get to a point where we understand that we *must* deal with our own mistakes. However, I'm not sure that is entirely possible until we work through a little of the pain that has shaped us. For this reason, today, we are going to look at a time when we may have been betrayed. You know I'm going to ask, so go ahead and write out any betrayal that still has the power to break you when your thoughts linger too long in the past. _____

_____

_____

_____

_____

_____

We do not have to be talking about sexual abuse alone. I will share with you one utterly wrong, for a lack of better words, betrayal from one woman's past:

> *The only thing I ever wanted in life as a child was a mother. Could she hold me, please, when I was scared? Could she sing to me in her sweet voice? Please, could she love me? Could she just look at me and smile? For some reason, she could do none of these things for her daughter, but for her son she could move mountains. She enjoyed telling me how they would leave me in my crib as an infant when I would not stop crying and just go to the park across the street. She thought it was funny when she declared that they would make sure to stay gone until they knew I would be asleep. When I got older they took great delight in being cruel to me. They hung my stuffed animals by their necks on the ceiling fan. They would tell me that I was such a bad mommy my animals committed suicide. And they would laugh while I attempted to get the animals down. They did many more things. Their cruelty nearly broke me. I did not have a single friend to turn to. I had a monster for a father. I **should have** had a mother. My brother **should have** been*

taught how to love his sister. I did not have these things that
so many people take for granted. I had betrayal. I had pain.
But I also had God. When I didn't even know what I needed,
He heard me in the groaning of my heart. We all have God.
He taught me how very wrong my family was. He showed
me how to love my children. Sometimes, when I look at my
children, when I hear them laugh, I can really see what I lost
in my childhood. I never want their eyes to hold that pain.

Did you recognize the Scripture she quotes? If not, turn
to Romans 8:26 and fill in the blanks: "In the same way, the
_____ helps us in our _____. We
do not _____ what we ought to _____ for,
but the _____ _____ intercedes for us
with _____ that _____ cannot express."
When we are so lost, confused, and hurt that we have no idea of
what we need, the Spirit of God intercedes for us. In this way we are
not crushed beneath the pain we feel when we can feel nothing else.
The Spirit not only intercedes for us, but *groans from the pain with us.*
Have you ever seen a loved one hurting and it made you hurt? Did
you just want to reach out to them and pull them close to you? Give
them comfort? Share your strength? _____

_____

When that woman we just heard from was lying abandoned in
her crib, the fear and pain she felt did not suffocate her. She was
able to love deeply and securely once again because God Himself
was her buffer against the cruelty. She did not know it for a while,
and she lived a very hard life for years. Then, one day, she chose to
believe God's truth over Satan's lies. TRUTH: *only God* can reach
the depths of pain and confusion caused by physical, mental, and
sexual abuse.

David was able to choose truth instead as well. In Psalm 55, he
cried his heart out to God about the anguish of betrayal. We talk a
lot about King David. Some things about him are not so pretty to
look at, but isn't that truth, also? No perfect feet walk this land. We
are all capable of making mistakes that hurt us and others around us.

What David is hailed for is his transparency, his honest repentance, and his devotion to the Lord, even when he fails miserably. David pours out his soul to God, and then ends his prayers with praise to the Lord alone. Turn to Psalm 55 and read it in its entirety.

Notice how David is praying to God in the first eleven verses, and then, when he hits the point of his greatest pain, the focus shifts. He is speaking, in verses 12-14, to the betrayer. Can't you see the look on his face when he says, "But it is you, a man like myself, my companion and my close friend...."? Look back to verse 2 and read again David's mindset. The NASB reads, "I am restless in my complaint and am surely distracted." Do pain and anger not have an uncanny ability to distract us from all else? If Satan can keep us in this state of mind, we will miss all the good things in our life. This kind of unrest causes children to wonder who in the world they are. It ends marriages and creates eating disorders and unstable mental conditions. It sends a lonely girl into the arms of a male who does not care for her on any emotional level (but the attention he gives her body fools her into imagining that he really cares for her). Confusion turns a sweet child into that teenager you won't let your kids near who lurks in shadows at the mall. Satan can twist a weave so cunning it forever ends relationships, altering hearts and minds, if we allow. In this way Satan takes and takes from us. This is how he tells us that no one can *really* love us. This is so exhausting!

Have you ever noticed that when you are upset, *everything* seems to be going wrong? _____

David wants to flee all that he knows to get away from the problem. Has this ever been the way you attempted to deal with problems? _____

You may get a *temporary* reprieve from the issue, but it does not vanish simply because you are no longer looking at it. You may be attempting to ignore something right now. Please pray for the courage to face it.

Next, David wishes for a fast display of God's wrath. But, by verse 16, his returned focus on God reminds him of God's *ultimate* protection. He remembers once again that judgment is the Lord's. Then, finally, David reconfirms that his trust is placed in God. Only at this final point in David's turmoil is he able to rest. He *knows* that his prayers are being heard (v. 17). He *knows* that constant prayer and focus on God are the keys to getting through the awful ordeal he is facing (v. 17). Let us get one thing clear, though: God is not a Band-Aid. He does not deliver quick fixes. God offers unchanging, uncompromising truth that, once accepted, changes the way we deal with situations.

This is a good time to talk about "defense mechanisms." David was greatly harmed when his "no" was not heard by his close companion—his "no" being of the nature that says, "No, my friend, do not betray me." If you were sexually abused, your "no" was blasted through—the "no" that said, "No, do not touch me." "No, do not harm me." We are going to look at that in the lesson tomorrow, but today we will open up defense mechanisms. These little buggers are used so very often. Here are some examples of what I am talking about:

__ **Denial:** Absolute refusal to face the facts.* If I don't look at it, then it will go away. Easy as pie. (Sure it is.)

__ **Repression:** Just block it out altogether.* Sometimes things are too painful for you to function, so your mind puts them in a box in a forgotten corner. God will cover these places as well, when the time is right.

__ **Regression:** Reverting back to an old way of doing things.* We talked about this last week.

__ **Reaction Formation:** Lying about how you really feel in order to avoid confrontation.*

__ **Sublimation:** Engrossing yourself in one activity to avoid thinking about something else.*

__ **Projection:** Putting the blame on someone else to get it off of you.* An example would be a spouse saying, "You never listen to me." "You always flirt with people." "You never do what I ask you to do."—but all the while it is the accusing spouse who does these things.

__ **Rationalization:** Explaining one's actions away.* "I *know* I did not have the money to buy that shirt *but* it was on a really great sale."

---

* Don H. Hockenbury and Sarah E. Hockenbury, Discovering Psychology: Fourth Edition (New York: Worth, 2007).

__ **Bullying:** Being so aggressive that the original offense is covered in a fear of the bully and no longer looked at.* Sometimes this tactic is effective enough that the wronged party is so confused they are not sure what happened in the first place or whose fault is whose.

__ **Blame Shifting:** Much like projection, this tactic is used to take all repercussions of the deed off of the person who actually did wrong. "If you wouldn't act like that, I wouldn't yell at you." "It wasn't my fault, it was your mom's." Et cetera, et cetera.

__ **Refusal to say I'm sorry:** This is just another way someone refuses to *take responsibility*.

Check off with one mark or color the things you have seen yourself do. Then go back and check off in another mark the things you have seen another do. Now, one last time, underline what the person who abused you did to cover or deny their wrongs. The point of this exercise is to focus on the many, many ways Satan attempts to work in people's lives. Each one of these actions is done in an attempt to avoid confrontation, cover up a wrong, and confuse a situation and the people involved. I put less sinister examples in the explanations but I am sure many of you can remember much worse. The woman in today's lesson was told that she was a really bad baby and that's why she was abandoned. She was later told that she was an annoying child and that's why her family was mean to her. Can you find ANY possible truth in those statements? _____

_____

We must get to the point, like she did, where we put all the pieces together and see clearly where Satan's lies are crouching. We use things like defense mechanisms to protect ourselves or try to control a situation. We use them to try to force the outcome we want. When we deal with situations in this way, we are falling into Satan's trap. This kind of behavior, on any level, is where he thrives. The people who abused you were putty in Satan's hands. But you and I are called to handle life differently.

Summarize Ephesians 4:22-24 here: _____

_____

_____

Summarize Ephesians 4:25-28 here: _____

_____

_____

One more, Ephesians 4:29-32 here: _____

_____

_____

Growing in this way can be challenging at best, excruciating at times, but liberating in the end. We have to begin to see ourselves not as women of abuse but as women. We have been betrayed, hurt, mocked, abandoned. We need healing for that, and have no doubt, we will receive it. But we are human also. We have, at some time, hurt others with our actions. We have held grudges or tried to punish offenses. We have been judge, jury, and, at times, tried to carry out a sentence or two. We need forgiveness for our mistakes. And make no mistake, we will receive it. Both sides of this coin are equally important. We need the power of God to move past the abuse and we need that same power to move on from our own mistakes. God wants to heal *all* of your scars.

Close today with: Ephesians 1:17-20. "I keep asking that the God of our Lord Jesus Christ, the glorious Father, may give you the *spirit of wisdom*, so that *you may know Him better*. I pray also that the *eyes of your heart may be enlightened* in order that you may *know the hope to which He has called you*, the riches of His glorious inheritance in the saints, and *His incomparably great power for us who believe*. That power is like the working of His mighty strength which He exerted in Christ when He raised Him from the dead."

What do you need this power to help you with?

_____

_____

_____

_____

Can I Ever Trust Again?

The work we will be doing this week, for many of you, will build foundations for your healing and growth. For the rest of you, this week will work to determine where the cracks in a previously solid foundation lay. This is critical in the process of choosing to believe in Truth instead. In order to grow, we must first realize that growth *is* needed. Then we must find out *where* growth is needed. This week will speak to all of you on different levels. Some of you have had childhoods so abusive and unstable that you have been left feeling like a stranger, ignorant and confused. Don't take that statement the wrong way. Ignorance is simply a lack of knowledge in one area or another. Ignorance is by no means stupidity or meant to be an unkind description of someone. If you had great parents and you are working through this study, that means that somewhere along the road an earthquake came along and shook your foundation. What we will attempt to do this week is highlight where important growth is needed, at different stages in life, and to explore what happens when that growth is compromised. Today we will look at two crucial boundaries formed in childhood.

BONDING IN INFANCY:

Can you imagine what happens inside a tiny heart when they are never picked up gently and nestled close? The sound of a mother's heartbeat and the scent of her skin represent safety, security, and comfort to an infant. The baby learns in these first few months that the world they have come into is a *good* place. That is a very simply put, yet utterly deep, truth. What do you think happens in an infant's heart and mind when they are not given this basic foundation?

_____

_____

_____

Do you think maybe they do not learn to trust from day one?

_____

When this happens to a person, every time someone betrays their trust, it just confirms what they have always known to be true in their lives. They come to *expect* betrayal. Satan's dark whispers are spoken powerfully in their ears—lies that say, "Everyone will betray you."

How about this: Do you think they *ever* feel safe? _____

_____

Could this be where deep feelings of loneliness come from?

_____

Can you relate to this in any way? How? _____

_____

Now, this foundation *can be* repaired with powerful, patient, consistent care. Many children who saw no love for some length of time before they were adopted or their parent chose to care for them grow to be healthy, stable, and happy adults. *Never* underestimate the healing power of *unconditional love.* Do you feel that you were ever loved unconditionally by anyone—a parent, friend, grandparent, teacher, husband, anyone? Who? Why? _____

_____

_____

How did that affect your outlook on life? _____

_____

_____

Did that love give you hope? Comfort? A feeling like you were not alone? Did it make you feel like no matter what happened you were going to be okay because someone had your back?[1] _____

_____

What does Joshua 1:5 say about bonding with God? _____

_____

What does Hebrews 13:5 say about the same? _____

_____

When we turn away from whatever keeps our attention from God and focus on the promises in His Word, we are able to be content with what He has given us. No matter what our pasts hold, we can find power in the next statement made in Hebrews 13:6. Please write this verse and pray for the confidence to claim it. ____

_____

_____

"MINE": OWNERSHIP/STEWARDSHIP

When infants turn into toddlers, the stage that most parents would happily skip over (if that little child were not so darn cute) is equally important. Toddler time brings about an understanding that something *belongs* to the child.[2] We as humans have to be able to say that something is "mine." This is "my home," "my child," "my work," "my favorite outfit," "my body," "my God," "my car, yard, belongings, friends, parents, job, money, church, voice." The list is endless, but the list begins in the toddler stage with simpler "my" things. Toddlers claim ownership over parents, toys, blankets— things of that nature. What happens when ownership is established correctly is that a sense of responsibility and attachment is formed.[3] Toddlers are taught to take care of their toys (responsibility), to ask for things they want (respect and kindness), to share things with

1. Dr. Henry Cloud and Dr. John Townsend, Boundaries: *When to Say Yes, How to Say No* (Grand Rapids: Zondervan, 1992).
2. Ibid.
3. Ibid.

others (selflessness). They are taught to not worry that they will lose the toy forever (security and relinquishing of control). In this way, we learn to take care of what is "mine" because we value it. What do you think happens when nothing is allowed to become "mine?"

_____

_____

What do you think happens when a child's body is not allowed to be theirs alone? Do you think maybe this leads to early sexual activity and/or promiscuity? Could this lead to confusion about what is and what is not appropriate sexually? _____

_____

Could this also lead to a lack of understanding about how to take care of one's body? _____

Look up 1 Corinthians 6:18-20. What do these verses say our bodies are? _____

These verses state that our bodies are meant not only for us, but to be a place for God to reside as well. This "temple" is to be a place where the Holy Spirit can resonate in man's entire being and speak to us. The verses also acknowledge that sexual actions go much deeper than we may have realized.

Deep connections are made when a sense of belonging is established. You _take care of something_ that is yours. You _spend time with it_ and enjoy being around it. You _treat it like it is important._ You see the _value_ in it. Let's take a few steps and recognize how damaging it is to a person when ownership is distorted or confused. What do you think happens when a child never feels like they belong to someone? _____

_____

Maybe they feel like they have to fend for themselves. Maybe they go in search of someone to belong with, skipping from one dysfunctional, unsatisfying relationship to the next. Do they have anywhere to go for help when they need something? Maybe they never understand that when something belongs to you, you take care of it. Do they learn how to respect anything? Do they learn how to find the true value in what and who is in their lives? Do they know they are important, significant? No one ever found value in them so what *is* value? Why is it valued? Can you hear the questions that can form in the mind of a child without this fundamental stage of development? Children have no ability to find the answer to these questions on their own. This lack of understanding just adds to a child's confusion. Have you ever felt this way? _____

_____

If we break this down by gender, some interesting things become clear. Boys, for the greater part of society, are raised to be strong and protective leaders and fixers. They are taught to take care of their families, to work hard to provide for them. What do you think happens in a young boy's mind when he is not taught these things? _____

_____

If a young man is never taught how to take care of something or that he is *capable and worth being a leader or provider*, the exact opposite of these qualities often grow in him. This kind of childhood can create the father who doesn't pay his child support, or the husband who is never physically satisfied with his wife. He can grow to become the man who never takes care of or protects anything. These are just a few examples.

When girls are not allowed their "mines," the nurturing, comforting, stable qualities of a woman may not be formed. The mother that leaves her child wherever she can so that she can go out for the night is created. Selfishness and dissatisfaction can be born here in abundance. She may always be driven to search for her worth, to belong somewhere; often in the arms of any willing man at nearly any cost.

If you are not heard, do not matter, are not loved, have nothing that belongs to you, then what the heck are you? Have you ever felt this way? When? Why? _____

_____

_____

When this happens, how in the world can we expect someone to grow into a selfless, responsible, caring, honest adult? How will they ever learn to trust again? The woman in day one would have to believe that, because she had a terrible mother she was doomed to become a terrible mother. She would have had to live her entire life thinking she was unlovable. Maybe you had a good childhood but somewhere along the road these two boundaries were attacked. Do you know how important you are? _____

Are you able to trust freely? _____

_____

What would happen to us if God did not look upon us and declare, "She is MINE"? We are so carefully kept because we belong to someone who loves us; someone who will exert every effort in order for us to *know* that we belong to Him. Do you KNOW that you belong to Him? _____

Look up Isaiah 43:1. Pause here before reading on. In this verse God declares you to be _____. Now read verses 2-7 and know that God is with you through whatever fire you walk in. You may not feel like you can trust again, but the more you feel the love of your Savior with you, you will be able to. Trust is scary by nature. It implies the possibility of being betrayed. This is true for humans but not for God. God does not betray. God does not forsake those who walk with Him. God is bigger than anyone who might ever betray you.

Turn to Joshua 3 and read this short chapter about the trust that God asked of His people and how He rewarded them. What did Joshua tell the people to do in verse 5? _____

_____

What happened in verses 15-16 when the waters were at their highest point of the year and crossing the river seemed impossible?

_____

_____

What picture forms in your mind when you read verse 17?

_____

God asked His people to trust Him to get them across the flooded Jordan. They needed only to put their toes in the water, to take that first step, and then God did the rest. He carried them through. He gave them a firm dry place to stand against a current powerful enough to carry them away. God offers this to you as well. You need only put your toe in the water. Yes, you can trust again because God wants you to have wonderful relationships. You can risk this part of yourself because no matter what man does to you, God is with you. He pours unconditional, never-ending, love onto you.

If you are never able to give your heart to a loved one or a friend completely, you will never know the joy God desires for your life. You simply cannot be halfway someone's wife or true friend. Just like we do not halfway belong to God. God does not base His relationship with us on our ability to never betray Him, because we will betray His truth, repeatedly. He bases it on His love for us, and we can do the same. We can base *everything* we do, *every person* we have a relationship with, on God's love for us.

Your "river Jordan" has nothing on God when you put your trust in Him. Do you want to allow the past to forever color your future? _____

_____

_____

_____

I know it is hard to risk your heart in this way. You cannot control what other people do, but there is so much joy out there waiting for you. Don't throw it away because someone else chose to hurt you. They were not listening to God's truth at that time. They were, and may still be, just as lost as anyone who listens to the lies Satan traps people in. You are worth so much more than that. The moment I was able to trust without reservation was the moment fear stopped controlling me. I was only able to do this when I knew that God was bigger than my past, and that He would never leave me to this world alone. I pray this understanding for you.

Guarding Your "House," Part 1

Today we will focus on how to build your boundaries up and secure your "house." I would highly encourage you to read the book *Boundaries: When to Say Yes, How to Say No* by Cloud and Townsend. Yesterday's lesson was based on some teaching from that biblically based book. We only touched on two of the most fundamental boundaries learned in childhood, but it would be beneficial to expand on that teaching.

Many women who suffer from abuse have distorted views about how to go on with everyday life. Do you have to please everyone, and how far should you go to please them? Can you stand up for yourself? Can you say no? Do you always get involved with the wrong kind of people? Do you jump in headfirst without thinking things through? Are you ever able to tell someone honestly how you feel? Do you struggle with controlling your thoughts, sexual in nature or otherwise? Do you still feel as if the abuse defines who you are? These are some of the things strong boundaries help people sort through. If you have never felt like *you* owned *you* and your voice mattered, this next exercise could be good for you.

In the space provided below, draw a picture of a house as if you were looking down through the roof into it. Include the basic front and back doors, windows, and yard. Do not put a fence around the yard yet. Leave out the mailbox, also. Make sure you leave a little room for workspace, because we are going to be adding some things inside and outside of your house as we go. The drawing will help you visualize what we are going to be talking about.

I hope I left you enough room.

Okay, so here we have a basic house. It looks pretty open huh? This is your house. But this is your house without boundaries. (I am getting a strange mental picture of that old commercial with the guy standing over the frying pan saying, "This is your brain...") Okay, back on track now. This "house" is going to represent you, your body, your mind, and your heart. Right now, your house is open to anyone passing through the neighborhood, so we need to build up some protections. You may need a little help with this. If truth be told, we all do from time to time. A storm like no other came and tore your house to pieces. It's a good thing that when we invite God in He gives us back everything that was taken.

Let your house lay there for a minute and turn to Luke 11:21-23. In this passage, Jesus teaches us a little something about our "houses." A strong man (Satan) came into someone's house and took ownership. Doesn't that sort of feel like what happens when you are attacked, or when you find yourself going through something really terrible? Someone saunters on up and takes whatever they want and pushes you right out of *your* house. I believe the ultimate goal of Satan is to occupy everyone's house. We would all be lost to him if there were not someone stronger around to fight for us.

What does verse 22 say? _____

_____

I bet you can guess who the "someone stronger" is? _____. What is even better about this passage is that it contains a promise. Jesus says that once He comes in and overpowers Satan for you, He will take back all that Satan stole from you. When we invite Jesus into our house, *He gives us back what was taken.* What was taken from you that you would really like to have back? Be specific. A relationship, your sanity, a feeling of safety, a peaceful night's rest, comfort in your skin, your joy, *any* joy, hope, innocence, a whole heart, trust, the ability to open up, the ability to deal with a difficult situation without completely stressing out, the simple ability to talk about something, the knowledge that you are not alone? _____

_____

_____

Remember that we only have control over our own choices and God does not force anyone to feel a certain way. God will not make someone treat you differently, but He will help you deal with whatever comes.

I came across a beautiful testimony of a time when God gave someone back a feeling and understanding of innocence. Allow me to share a personal word:

God asked of me two very specific things when I began to write this study. One of those things was to hold myself to a level of sexual purity that I had never known before. I cannot remember a time when my life was not influenced by some way, shape, or form of sexual behavior. I never knew innocence, or even why it was important. I had never known the sweet fluttering of a stomach's first crush. I did not understand that a girl could have a relationship with a boy without any sexual overtones or expectations. I did not see myself apart from what men had taken from me and forced upon me. I was not gifted with the terrifying, exciting wedding-night jitters. One time in yet another new high school, I entered a classroom and a boy looked at me and said, "I'm going to call you 'Abused', because you just look abused." I was never just a girl: I was "Abused."

When I began to write this study, I made a commitment to any woman who would go through this material, and to God, that I took/take very seriously, so I put off watching any television or movies that had any sort of sexual content. I had to mind what I read and the conversations I took part in. I tried to be conscious of my body language and clothing. This was very difficult, because we live in an EXTREMELY sexual world. I prayed that God would quiet the sexuality inside me so that I could follow this request He had made of me. I thought this purity was necessary for the Bible study, so that my mind could be focused on this work, and on one hand that is true. On the other hand, God was giving me back an understanding of the innocence that was taken from me. I began to feel a peace inside myself that I had never known before. My days began to be days without any sexual overtone, as I imagine a child's life should be—free of sexual influence that will take from the natural development and beauty of a child. I would never have held myself to this standard of purity on my own, but I am so thankful that God asked this of me. He has shown me ME apart from the sexual world. I began to know myself in a way that I had yet to uncover. This is a gift I cannot fully explain.

Please understand this is not a call for "nuns are us." I still desire to enjoy a healthy marriage someday, but I think this understanding of youthful innocence was a critical part of my healing. Sexuality is meant to be a beautiful and natural part of being a woman. But how can women know this if they have never understood innocence? My house was once built on a sexual foundation, but no longer. No, now my house is my own. *I* choose what comes in and goes out of my house.

Do you remember innocence? If so, what was that time like for you? _____

_____

Luke 11:34 talks about our "vision" being either clear—which makes our bodies full of light—or being full of darkness. We are greatly influenced by what we see. The importance of sexual purity in childhood foundations cannot be overstated. As we grow, this aspect of life is (and should be) introduced to us, but never in a harmful way. Look up Song of Solomon 2:7. What does the verse say about this topic? _____

_____

The fact that sexual arousal should not happen too early is repeated three times in Song of Solomon; here in 2:7, again in 3:5, then again in 8:4. If you were to read this book of the Bible through, it would be hard to argue that physical intimacy between married couples is not meant to be a wonderful part of the equation. But when anything is repeated three times in Scripture, there must be an important reason for the repetition. (If you do read this book, make sure to read a biblical commentary on the verses, because some of the language can be a bit confusing.)

The only additions we will make to our drawings today are the inner rooms of our houses. Go back and draw the basic innards of your house. Make sure you draw your bedroom and any other bedrooms with doors.

Let's close today in thought about why purity is such an important part of a child's foundation and how difficult it is to maintain purity in our world today. We will never be children again, but we may have children of our own one day, and we need to understand how these things can affect them. If we do not have our own children, we may be in a position someday where we need to pass this guidance on. God is also waiting to show us the truth where sexual behavior is concerned. God created this part of us. Let us learn from Him what He intended in this area.

How do you think sexual influences influence young children?

_____

_____

_____

Take just one minute to look around your everyday world and make a list of every place that you see a sexual reference. (For example: TV commercials, radio, billboards, the way clothing is styled today, magazines at the checkout stand, the crude humor of people you may know) _____

_____

_____

How did those things influence you when you were young?

_____

_____

_____

How do they influence you now? _____

_____

_____

Why do you think we put doors on the rooms in your house?

_____

_____

Do you believe that God will give back the things that Satan has taken from you? _____

Have you experienced this yet? When? How? _____

_____

_____

_____

_____

_____

_____

_____

_____

_____

_____

_____

_____

_____

_____

_____

_____

_____

_____

Guarding Your "House" Part 2

L et's refresh our memories of where we were in yesterday's lesson. Go back to the Luke Scripture and read 11:21-23 again; then continue through verse 26. This passage also holds a warning—did you catch it in verses 24-26? _____

_____

_____

If we do not build defenses around our house, we are at risk of losing much more than we lost the first time. Have you ever known someone who fell off the wagon over and over, and each time they fell it seemed to get a bit worse, and then a bit worse, until you couldn't even recognize them any longer? _____

_____

We can start to build boundaries by putting up a fence around our yard. Go back to your drawing and add this feature. The fence will serve as a sign that you mean business. It means that you are beginning to believe that you are worth something. You are putting on some armor of your own. This armor must include Christ, or it will not stand. When Jesus fought Satan in the desert, do you know what His only weapon was? Check out Matthew 4:1-11. Out of everything Jesus had at His disposal, the only weapon He used against Satan was _____.

Scripture is also how Christ proclaimed who He was (Luke 4:16-21).

Scripture is also what gave Jesus comfort in times of stress. Look up Mark 15:25-34. Here, Jesus is suffering hours of physical pain and emotional torment. He says _____ _____ in verse 34. Do you think God actually forsook Jesus when it clearly states in His Word, "Never will I leave you; never will I _____ you" (Heb. 13:5)? Let's allow Psalm 22:1 to answer that question. What does this verse say? _____

_____

Jesus was quoting Scripture for comfort. If you have a minute, read through Psalm 22. These words seem to be written specifically for Christ at that very moment in His life. It is interesting to note that, when Psalm 22 was penned, the Romans had not even invented death by crucifixion yet.

God also uses Scripture to speak to and comfort us. Listen to this testimony:

> *I was turning eleven years old the first time I was raped. Every single birthday after that eleventh one brought the rapes back to me in vivid detail. I saw them, felt them, heard them, and hated them all over again. When I woke up on my twenty-seventh birthday, I prayed with all my heart that God would one day give me back my birthday. I prayed before I even opened my eyes, and then I got up and tried to pass the day as quickly as possible. I was mopping the kitchen floor when a friend came by unexpectedly. She had a simple gift for me. I had not told her the horrors this day held, but I was happy for the distraction. I set the gift bag on my lap and pulled out a decorative tile that had the words from Isaiah 41:10 on it. The tile said: **Fear not. I am with thee, for I am thy God. I will strengthen thee. I will help thee.***
>
> *No person heard my prayer that morning in my bed. But God heard. And with this Scripture, God answered my prayer with words of comfort and strength. With these words, He told me He was real and would help me. A few months later I asked my friend why she picked that gift for me. She told me that she was out one day, and when she saw it, she felt like God was telling her to get it for me. I am in my thirties now,*

and let me tell you that my birthdays are once again my own.
I praise the LORD for that!

That lady began to build her fence with the truth that is written in Scripture. What are your walls made of? Things people say about you? Things people try to get you to believe? Vices you try to use to cover up the emptiness? _____

_____

If you said yes to any of those "building materials," why don't you try out Scripture for a change? If people only knew the power that Scripture holds, they would never be the same. See, Satan knows the truth also. He may constantly try to undermine it, but when standing face-to-face with the Word of God, Satan knows he is defeated. The strongest boards of your fence are made out of Truth. The nails (the power) that hold them together were once used to hold Christ to very different set of boards.

Now, did you think to put a gate in your fence? If not, go back and do that, because you are not an island of one, my sister. Put a gate there so that you may CHOOSE who and what you let in your yard. A familiar verse for many people is Matthew 7:6, which talks about how we should not give the best of ourselves to someone who will just use and betray it. Also, there are definitely levels of closeness you should allow the people you know and meet. Write "acquaintances" outside your gate. Write "some friends" and "some family" inside the gate in your yard. This is as far as some people need to go, and that is perfectly fine. You *do not* have to allow everyone into your house. Yes, even some family members can stay outside. You *do not* have to say yes to everything that is asked of you. Your time is as precious as your house. You choose what to do with it. You are not being mean or bad by saying no sometimes. Saying no does not mean that you are not someone's friend or loved one. Take special note that we are not jumping off the cliff called "selfishness"—we are simply learning how to balance our time and efforts. Remember that when you give your life to God, you work for Him and not for man—thus, man's demands on you are greatly weakened.

Look up Colossians 3:23. What does this basically say? _____

_____

In the KJV, the words "with all your heart" are summed up in one word: "heartily." When I looked up the original language meaning of this word, I begin to really understand what God is telling us here. This word is used only once in Scripture, and it means that you should remember that what you do in this life is done for God, and that it should be done with every bit of the breath He breathed into you. The word "heartily" is broken into two Greek words: *ek* meaning "origin (the point whence motion or action proceeds)" and *psuche* meaning "breath (heart, life, mind, soul)." You do not work a little for God and a little for man. You either work for God OR man. Funny thing is, when you do God's work, it greatly benefits many people.

Now that we have the borders secured, we can work on the inside of the house. Draw your front door if you have not already, and write "close friends" and "some family" inside your house. These are the people you feel the most comfortable with. They are safe to be this close to you, because you trust them. Believe it or not, there are some God-honoring people out there whom you will be able to trust. Remember also that there is such a thing as having unrealistic expectations of someone. Sometimes we want so badly for someone to be that one person who will never fail us that we are crushed when they do. People are not made to be perfect. You cannot expect or even hope that someone will *never* do something wrong. You have got to learn to give the same grace to others that God gives to all of us. What does Ephesians 4:32 say? _____

_____

It is simply not fair to expect perfection, and when a trusted friend or loved one lets you down, it does not mean they are just like everyone who has ever hurt you. Their faults do not give you license to write them off. They just mean that they are human. If they consistently and unrepentantly hurt you, time and again, then you may need to distance yourself from them—but that is an entirely different story than a friend making a mistake.

Have you ever found yourself having unrealistic expectations of someone? _____

Has anyone ever accused you of making those kinds of demands? Who? When? _____

Make sure you write your name and (if you have a spouse) your spouse's name inside your bedroom. If you are not married, this section is still important for you to understand how physical intimacy in marriage should be. This room of your house is only big enough for two. The relationship you share with your spouse should be different from any other relationship you have. You literally become one when you enter into that covenant agreement—ONE, not two, or three, or four (Matt. 19:4-6). No extra bodies in the bed or on the television, in the form of pornography or person. Many, many, people struggle with this truth, and really, when you take a look around, you can hardly blame them. Most of today's entertainment screams promiscuity and homosexuality. This can be even more challenging for a person with abuse in their history, because total confusion may have taken over this area.

Hebrews 13:4 in the NASB states: "Marriage is to be held in honor among all, and the marriage bed is to be undefiled." Does this make any sense to you? _____

When another partner is brought into the picture, what that really means is that the one spouse is not enough to satisfy the other.

Ephesians 5:22-33 talks about how husbands and wives should treat each other. Nothing is hidden from a spouse. They alone should see and feel and know all of you. They are special in this way. This is one of the main things that set your relationship apart from all others. How special are your secrets when they are shared with multiple partners?

Let's pause here for a second. Has anyone ever told you that it is okay for your husband to desire you in a sexual way? Please be honest in answering these next questions. Have you ever felt uncomfortable with displays of your husband's sexual desire? _____

_____

Are your memories of the abuse still connected to any sexual act or comment? _____

When your husband looks at your body, he should be looking at you with love and desire. *He is not* the person who looked at you with evil. (If your husband has harmed you in this way, please seek biblical counsel and advice! This is *not okay* just because you are bound in marriage!) My prayer for you is that you will be able to separate the abuse from what you should be able to freely enjoy with your spouse. I have experienced this healing. I know it is possible. Write out any questions or concerns you have about this topic and bring them with you to group. Is there a certain body language or body motion, a certain saying or phrase, a song perhaps, that makes you remember those awful events? Do not be embarrassed or worry what someone will think of your questions. If Satan can keep you trapped here, your healing will never be complete. If we can isolate the things that cause the flashback, then we can combat the problem in that area. We can pray specifically for healing and truth to blast away the conflict.

Finally, put a mailbox outside your fence. Your mailbox can hold accusations against you made by other people. You do not need to automatically believe everything that someone says to or about you but you do need to honestly assess the situation. Is it possible that you did something wrong? If so, you need to take ownership of your actions. That piece of mail needs attention, but you can make cute little paper airplanes out of the junk mail and go enjoy a windy day.

We have done a lot of work today. This is difficult building, I know, but your healing is more than worth a little sweat. The drawing of your house is just a simple way to help you visualize and gain a bit of understanding about healthy boundaries. I very much hope this lesson has helped you in some way. I pray for each and every woman who will ever touch this study. There is a wonderful, strong, beautiful, free, entirely unique and special person that God created in you. The abuse has tried to take her from you, but God is here to give you everything back. Go to Him. Believe in Him. He will show Himself to every willing heart.

Lord, help us to know You. Help us to understand Your truth. In Christ's name I pray, Amen.

DAY 5

God's Boundaries

Today we are going to step on heaven's side of the fence for a view of some of God's boundaries. God has characteristics like no other, and the better we understand those characteristics, the better we will understand and be able to accept our Lord and what He teaches. We would need another whole study to look at the many characteristics and boundaries of God, so we are only going to touch on the ones that appear most relevant to our topic. Before we begin, take a breath, and say a little prayer asking God to show Himself to you today in a way that you have never known Him. Remember that our ultimate goal here is to separate the abuse, and the effects of the abuse, from the women that we are in Christ. When I say "in Christ," I mean in the life you have chosen to follow God with, and in the Truth that Christ is. Many people find God through healing. That is my prayer for you, my dear sister.

"Easy" is the last word I would expect to be attributed to this study, and I know one reason for the difficulty is the nature of the questions I have to ask you. My intent is never to harm you or push you back into a memory, but to guide you onto a path of healing. With this in mind, I have to ask if you have a block in your mind or in your heart against calling God your Father. Was your father the source of your abuse? _____

Maybe it was not your father himself, but he allowed the abuse to happen. If the answer to either of those questions is yes, then I completely understand if you have an issue thinking of God as your Father. In reality, God is your Creator. He is your Father. But He IS NOT your earthly father. If your father abused you, then he did not truly follow God. We need to understand that God is the ultimate example of fatherhood, and His role is nothing like we may have ever known.

In Isaiah 63:16, the prophet Isaiah understood that, even if our earthly fathers abandon or harm us, God is still out true father. Read this verse and try to understand what is being proclaimed here. The New American Standard reads: ". . . though Abraham does not know us and Israel does not recognize us . . ." That word "recognize" stands out to me when I read this verse because any man who would harm his child does not recognize who and what that child is. They do not recognize who and what they are supposed to be to that child. Isaiah 63 and 64 are a plea to God for redemption because the prophet recognized how lost the people were without God.

If this does not pertain to your situation, kindly allow your sisters a word of prayerful, comforting testimony from the same woman who shared her birthday gift with you in day four:

Every time I said the word "father," I saw my father's face. I heard his laugh as he beat me. I smelled the alcohol on his breath when the memory was particularly sharp. I could not bring myself to even think of God as my Father. They were polar opposites. One day in Sunday school, I was stricken by the love on one woman's face as she openly prayed to her Father God. I knew right then I would never know God on any deeper level until I could get past this block. A few weeks later, I found the sanctuary of our church empty, and I lay on the steps of the altar and prayed very simply for help. Thinking back on that moment now, I think He was just waiting for me to ask. A peace came over me the likes of which I can't explain. I didn't hear a word, but I felt like I was resting my tired soul against His strong shoulder. I felt, for the very first time in my life, what a child is supposed to feel when her father puts his

arm around her. I felt protected. God has been my Father since
that day. If you are reading this I pray with all my heart this
freedom for you.

We also need to understand that God is the epitome of
PATIENCE. We will fail in our attempts at righteousness, as
we are humans. We may lose faith in moments of distress. We
most definitely will require God to remind us repeatedly of His
power and that He is real. Our broken hearts will need application
after application of His matchless love, and we will utterly fail in
understanding that love from time to time. But we do not need to
fear that God will throw lightning at us when we do fail.

Two Scriptures that I found sum this truth up beautifully:
Nehemiah 9:16-21, which speaks of God's great patience towards
His people in the Old Testament, and 2 Peter 3:8, 9, which explains
God's patience towards us in the New Testament. In the words of
2 Peter 3:8, 9, God is not slow in keeping His promise to judge
each and every man, "He is _____ with _____. "
He treats you this way because He does not wish to lose you. When
you stumble, do not give up. Do not hide. Just try again. Write your
name in the blank here because this promise is every bit as much for
you as for anyone else: "He is patient with _____."

God's patience shows God's WILLINGNESS to be involved
in your life. Do you remember reading Isaiah 1:18, where God
asks to talk with you, to help you make sense of this life? God says
"_____ let us _____ together . . ." Here, and in
many other places in the Word, God is asking to have a relationship
with you.

In Job 10:1-7, when Job asks God, "Do you have eyes of flesh?
Do you see as a mortal sees?" these are telling accusations of a
man in despair. How often do we say, "How could anyone know
what I am going through?" Unless you have walked in someone's
shoes, you really don't completely understand what they are going
through. Although I do not believe God is limited in this way, I
think He knew that our connection with Him would be limited
until we could see that He truly does understand what it means to
have "eyes of flesh" and the limits of a human. He was willing to

put on flesh and live as a man so that we would *know* that He has walked in our shoes—so that we could claim Hebrews 4:15. He even came to us in the least threatening way possible: as an infant.[4] It is like He wanted to eliminate any possible fear factor. Every time man encounters God or an Angel of the Lord in the Old Testament, the command "Fear not" stands before the scene. If He came as God in all His power and glory, who would ever be brave enough to sit and have dinner with Him? Who would be able to laugh with Him and ask Him the hard and honest questions?

Of course, there are a few things that God is NOT WILLING to let slide. When Jesus forgave sin, He never made excuses or downplayed the sins. He simply acknowledged the sinner and forgave the willing heart. Look up Luke 7:36-50 for one excellent example.

God is also not willing to allow us to hold onto grudges or hate each other. What does Jesus say to do concerning this matter even before He will accept your worship in Matthew 5:21-24?

_____

God knows what anger and bitterness will cost you. He will not allow us to remain unchanged when we come to know Him. Slowly but surely, the way we handle situations should become more mature and graceful.

Finally, God is a GIFT-GIVING God. Did you know that?

_____

He gives in so many ways—sometimes spiritual, sometimes material, sometimes deeply personal gifts only you could possibly understand. Think on James 1:17: "Every good and perfect gift is from above, coming down from the Father of the heavenly lights, who does not change like shifting shadows."

If you have a problem accepting a gift, you are not alone. Many, many, survivors of abuse have been lured with "gifts" into the abuse or "rewarded" with "gifts" after the abuse. The sickness of Satan knows no bounds. Any and every good thing that God has made, Satan will attempt to distort and destroy. Has this ever been an issue for you? Why? _____

_____

_____

4. Philip Yancey, *The Jesus I Never Knew* (Grand Rapids: Zondervan, 1995).

God loves to give gifts. God's people love to give gifts. Giving is an expression of kindness and help. The giver of a true gift receives far more than they are giving away. Hear these words and read them over until they make absolute sense to your heart: A true gift does not come with strings attached. A true gift holds no expectations of payment in return. A gift is simply meant to be accepted and cherished for the kindness that gave the gift to you.

When I think about God's willingness to be involved in my life, I can't help but marvel at His AWESOMENESS. Whenever I begin to wonder about the reality of God, I go outside and look up. Hopefully, you did this exercise before you began this study. Even if you did, it would not hurt to go back outside and try to find some feasible explanation for outer space. As brilliant as man ever gets, we will never reach an understanding of space. We will never explain its boundaries.

Every time I hear about something awesome that happened that is beyond reason, my faith in God is strengthened. The testimonies I hear and read from others and the ones I have myself strengthen my belief in God. Is there any particular thing (something that amazes you—an event, a testimony, an inability to explain something) that strengthens your belief in God? _____

_____

_____

_____

_____

_____

_____

_____

_____

Week 6

Satan's Deeds / Invisible Ties / Resulting Sin

God's Promise: You will be separated from the abuser/s. The husband and wife shall become one.

Do you believe this? _____

Why? Why not? _____

_____

_____

Satan's Lie: You will always be tied to the abuser/s. Everyone is the same. Sex is only physical.

Do you believe this? _____

Why? Why not? _____

_____

_____

What Is and What Should Never Be

Here we are, pulling into week six, and you are still here, which means you have not given up, which means you are serious about wanting to move on from the past. I cannot express to you how thankful I am that this study is still in your hands. I wish you had never needed to touch this work, but we cannot change the past. We do, however, have the power to say where we go from here. Today you are still committed to moving forward. I rejoice with you! I wish I could see your precious face as you begin to realize just how important you are. After this week, there is only one week of study left. I am praying to walk with you to the very end.

I am going to try to keep this day's work as simple as possible. Please answer the questions the best you can, and remember that the point of these exercises is to help you be actively involved in this work. Sometimes just the act of saying a thing out loud or writing it down is a helpful way of getting the issue out on the table so it can be dealt with. I encourage you to keep writing in your journals. We do not want to miss a thing that needs to be brought to light.

Many people feel that if you have never had sex out of wedlock, with or without your consent, then you should skip topics like the one we will be opening up this week. My theory: if you are doing this study, then you already know the things you maybe should not know yet, and to leave a person uneducated is much more dangerous than attempting to shelter them. The best intentions come from good hearts, but we must look at the facts. Fact: you have been introduced to and/or harmed by sexual activity. Fact: you need to know what God intends in this area.

To once again cover the basic of basics, turn to Genesis 2 and read verses 24 and 25. What does this say to *you* personally? _____

_____

_____

The King James Version reads that the man "shall cleave unto his wife: and they shall be one flesh." Cleave literally means "to impinge, to adhere." Like superglue. Verse 25 also says that they were not ashamed to be naked in each other's presence. If you are married, are you this comfortable with your mate? _____

If you are or are not married, do you feel exposed when you are unclothed? Do you still feel as if someone is watching? _____

If Satan still has the power to trap you here in your own skin, I pray that by the end of this week he will be defeated. We still have some work to do, and it is not all pretty, but your courage has brought you this far.

Now, keep in mind that the covenant of marriage is sealed the moment intercourse occurs; it is this physical act that binds what the two hearts wish to do with the rest of their lives. This is one of the purposes of sexual activity. Another purpose is to enjoy intimacy with your spouse, to *know them as no other knows them,* and vice versa. The other purpose, of course, is to have children. Keep in mind also that one of Satan's greatest lies is that sex is only a physical act, with no lasting results and no emotional ties.

Have you ever felt as if you were still connected in some way to the person/people who abused you? _____

Does even the thought of being tied to them in any way repulse you? _____

I had a very hard time with this idea. I could not deny that, in my darkest hours, I could not seem to shake the feeling that the abuser's defilement was still with me—that they were still somehow on my skin. I hate to be so blunt, but these are the things no one ever wants to speak about. These are issues that are too easily kept in the dark. So, inviting Light into our work today, I will be blunt. You may not need to participate in all parts of today's lesson. You may just read the day's lesson and gain insight into how to help someone else in this area. Either way, you win today.

If I believe that intercourse creates a physical bond between willing partners, I cannot pretend that the act does not create some kind of tie, unwanted as it is, between any partners. (Look back on day four of week two to refresh your memory concerning this blood covenant.) What we are going to focus on today is separating this unwanted tie. When a person is raped, part of the rapist is physically left with them, and much of the rapist is mentally left with them. The same thing happens when any forced intimacy occurs. We see this theme again and again throughout our study: what God created for good Satan attempts to distort and destroy. Whatever action steps outside of God's will is named sin. Sin is not a standalone action, for sin bears fruit, just as love bears fruit. The fruits of sin are things like shame, guilt, anxiety, disgrace, pain and separation from God.

I have prayed many times to be cleansed of my own sins. I understood that concept. What I did not understand, for a long time, was the healing aspect of praying to be cleansed of another's sins. Just as Jesus bore sins done *by* me, he bore the sins done *to* me. No matter how you look at the issue, abuse leaves marks. The fruit of another person's sin was placed on your body. God will purify that sin as well. Have you ever prayed for purity in this way?

Turn to Psalm 51:10. What does this verse speak about?

Look also at Hebrews 1:3. What does this one say? _____

These verses speak of purity and renewal. You do not have to wear another's sins a moment longer. You need not be tied to the abusers in any way. The gift of bonding yourself with the man you give your heart to in marriage should be *yours and his alone*. If you have ever sat in the shower until you could no longer feel the water pounding on your skin in a desperate attempt to feel anything else, pray with me now to know this purity. If you have ever felt defiled, ruined, or any other terrible result of the abuse on your person, inside or out, pray with me now.

LORD, create in me a pure heart. Separate and free me from _____ (the abuser's) sins. Separate and free me from my own sins. Purify my body, LORD, and renew a steadfast spirit within me. In the name of Christ I pray, Amen.

By whatever means necessary—aside from harming yourself or someone else—remove yourself from the abuse. If you have photographs of the person who abused you, you don't have to keep those. You don't have to remain in any kind of contact with someone because of what someone else thinks or wants, such as a family member or an in-law. (It is perfectly OK to distance yourself from the person who abused you.) If you still have any of the clothes you wore at the time of the abuse, get rid of them. If you still have any of the "gifts" the abuser lured you in with or "rewarded" you with, toss those out too. As far as you can throw them is quite all right. Get alone and stand unclothed in front of a full-length mirror. Look at yourself and declare, "THIS IS NOT DIRTY!" Say it over and over until you begin to feel the truth in it. Close your eyes and mentally visualize yourself wiping the abuse off your skin and lifting it up to God or laying that darkness at the feet of Christ your Savior. He gave Himself as sacrifice for one of these very reasons. It is time, sister, for you to be free of this darkness.

When we accept the truth God teaches, we get to shuck the things that drag us down. Second Corinthians 5:17: "Therefore if anyone is in Christ, he is a new creature; the old things passed away; behold, new things have come" (NASB). The new does not cover the old up, it *replaces* the old. Do not abandon this prayer until you know the freedom of this truth. You don't have to use my words; you can pray your own. And please know that I am praying with you. _____

_____

_____

Signals and Stop Signs

We are going to do a little relationship driver's education, so to speak, today. I have yet to meet a woman who has abuse in her history and has not had any trouble at all with relationships. I will again attempt to keep this lesson pretty basic. Remember that this study is for all age groups, so kindly bear with your sisters through areas that do not pertain to you.

Becoming intimate with someone is a serious thing, to be approached with wisdom and caution. Our human feelings and desires can be so overwhelming that at times they seem to come out of nowhere with the speed of a freight train and flatten us midstep. Young or old, tempering that swift rise and fall of emotion can be one of the greatest challenges in our lives. At times, we will know without a doubt that we are not supposed to be involved with so-and-so. At other times, we will be positive that so-and-so hung the moon, only later to realize that what we thought was the moon turned out to be rotten, stinky cheese. I have known many women and teenage girls who have an ultimate driving need not to be alone. In this desperation, they attach themselves to the first man who comes along. The woman's desire to be noticed is so strong that the man's negative characteristics are more easily overlooked. When that relationship does not work out, they are crushed, but only long enough to find another man and repeat the cycle. In hopes that they will finally be loved and finally be enough for someone, they give that man every single thing they have. I have also met many daughters of those women, and their stories are heartbreaking. The daughters always have the same question in their eyes: "Why couldn't she focus on me a little bit?"

I know how hard it is to be alone. I was married for thirteen years when my husband left. He thought he had found something better, and I was dropped to scrape the pieces of my life back together. It would be so easy to find someone to fill that emptiness, but unless that person is brought to me by God, I am not willing to go through that cycle again. The divorce handed me a ticket for a crash course in the mystery of intimate relationships. Lesson one: I am worth more than being subject to someone else's all-consuming selfishness. I wish I had that wisdom from day one of those thirteen years.

Do you know this truth? Do you *know* that you are worth having someone's selfless love and devotion? _____

I do not want to hear you say something along the lines of "I deserve a poor relationship because I royally messed up a few times." I am going to let you in on a little secret: EVERYONE messes up, NO ONE deserves grace. That is why grace is such a precious gift. Simply put, God gives grace to repentant hearts. Accept it! Don't waste it. (I saw a sign once that made me grin. It said, "Don't judge me because I sin differently than you." The irony was that it was sitting on the desk of someone who really annoyed me. Gotta love The Big Guy's humor sometimes.)

Lesson two: if the relationship does not come from God, *it will* fail. In my marriage, I tried so hard. I spent so many tears in prayer, but in the end, this truth was an inflexible lesson learned.

Turn with me to Acts 5:29-39. Here is the litmus test to set all questions, all hopes, and all relationships by. What do verses 38 and 39 say? _____

_____

_____

_____

This truth was even recognized by a man who was not a follower of Christ. He was, however, a respected teacher of the law. His entire life had been spent studying the laws God gave to His people Israel. He learned how to recognize whether or not something came from God. If a relationship has to be forced, then there is an excellent chance that it is not going to last. Do you think a sudden infatuation with someone, originating from you or from the man, is going to turn into a lifelong partnership? _____

Do you think that, if you focus on a few nice qualities in him, all the negative ones will eventually see the light? Before you jump in headfirst, put that thing to the test. Whoever God gives you will be worth the wait. Let Him drive for a while. If you are a romantic like me, you could visualize this concept as enjoying a horse-drawn carriage ride with your honey. The path is a mystery, as we never know what tomorrow will hold. But the driver is God, so you can rest in the knowledge that He knows where He is going.

I hold a testimony close to my heart that I heard from one beautiful young woman. She struggles with loneliness, like so many of us. She never had a mother to teach her that she was special. She never had a father to show her that she should be protected. Sadly, she is one of many.

When I was attacked, my virginity was spared, though at the time I did not know it. I thought any sexual activity took a girl's virginity. I soon became sexually active of my own free will. When I lost my virginity, I knew only that the act itself was physically different than when I was attacked. No one ever taught me anything about being a woman. I didn't know why I felt emotionally connected to the guys. I didn't even know why there was blood that first willing time I was with a man. I didn't know that there was a part of myself that I could give to someone as a gift, much less that anything about me was special. I wish I had known what these things really meant. I thought sex was just sex. I thought if you didn't have sex with a guy, he would leave you. I found out they all left anyway, over and over. One day, I heard a woman talk about how special she felt on her wedding night. I felt cheated all over again. I will never get the virginity back, but I hope one day to know the deep soul connection of being intimate with a man who I actually love and who loves me back.

Now turn to Jude 16. This is a tiny little book right before Revelation. Jude speaks here about false teachers, but the characteristics they share with deceitful men are uncanny. What kind of person does Jude 16 describe to you? _____

_____

_____

Have you ever known a Jude 16 person? _____

When you see this kind of behavior in a man, your radar should be blinking a very pronounced caution signal! He's not just cute or rough around the edges; he should be holding the darn stop sign. Boasters and complainers are hardly enjoyable company. If a person finds fault in nearly everything around them, then there is surely some deep-seated dissatisfaction they have yet to deal with. Their "thorn in the flesh" may not even have a thing to do with you. We would also do well to be wary of an overly flattering tongue, because oftentimes, sweet words drip with false motives. The more confident you become in yourself, the more you will be able to sort the real compliments from the deceptions.

On the flipside: have you ever been a Jude 16 person? _____ When I ask you these kinds of questions, I am not being judgmental in any way, and I am not trying to make you feel bad about anything or air your dirty laundry. What I am trying to do is lead you into open honesty. No one on this earth is without fault. (I am not proud of many of the things I have done.) But no one will ever change without honesty—at the very least, between themselves and God.

We have talked about some basic signals and stop signs; now let's talk about one more very important signal. Fear is a great signal that tells you that there is a problem. Much like anger, fear is also a coat of many colors: fear of loss, fear of exposure, fear of putting yourself out there again, fear of repeated abuse; fear that all men are the same, fear, fear, fear... When you think about the relationship you are in, or may be in one day, what is your greatest fear? _____

_____

_____

Are you afraid he may one day find out about the abuse and it will alter your relationship? _____

These ideas are understandable from the viewpoint of where you have been. Just remember one thing, my dear friend: "There is no fear in love. But perfect love (love that comes from God) drives out fear . . ." (1 John 4:18). Someone that you are in an intimate relationship with should be someone that you feel safe enough with to tell anything. Secrets are like landmines that Satan is eagerly awaiting to explode at the worst possible moment. Take the power away from the wicked one and beat him to the punch. If God sent that man to you, then he will desire to protect you all the more.

Fear is also an emotional signal that should shine like a warning beacon in a relationship. If anything your partner does physically or mentally causes you to fear him or the situation you are in, then you need to take a big step back and think things through. Fear is NOT the way to get someone to do something you want them to do. Fear must not be the driving force in your relationship. If he raises his voice or his fist to make you "behave," then you need to seek counsel now. God teaches that a man should love his partner as he loves himself (Eph. 5:25-29). Remember that he cannot love you if he does not love himself, and you cannot love him if you do not love yourself. Sometimes, when fear is all we have known, these are hard truths to grasp.

If we had to rely on any one person to make everything right, we would be utterly lost. Your life is worth so much more than to be delivered over into the hands of wicked men. We are vastly limited in our views and understandings. Far too often, we see only what we wish to see—or what is big enough to block our vision. Thankfully, we are not expected to travel through life on our own strength. "God is our refuge and strength, an ever-present help in trouble. Therefore we will not fear . . ." (Ps. 46:1, 2). "We wait in hope for the LORD; He is our help and our shield. In Him our hearts rejoice, for we trust in His holy name" (Ps. 33:20, 21). Thank you, LORD, for your help. Thank you for your shield.

"Submission" Is Not Really a Four-Letter Word

A good deal of our study has been spent examining areas of physical relationships, because, for the most part, that is what was used to harm you. There are so many variations of sexual abuse. Every single person's story is different, so the best way I know how to go about seeking healing truths for the whole group is to begin in foundational truths. My prayer for you is that you'll use this study as a building block on your unique journey. We will look at marriage one more time today, because healing from sexual abuse and healthy marriages go hand-in-hand. Please do not enter into a marriage before you seek healing in this area! Satan will relentlessly use this part of your life to tear your marriage apart if he is allowed.

Do you have a problem with the idea of submission? Why? Why not? _____

_____

_____

_____

Does the very thought of submitting to someone else's needs or desires sometimes have the ability to throw you back into that place where you were forced to submit against your will? _____

_____

If you have struggled with this confusing battle inside you, do you think that it could be causing confusion between you and your spouse? Have you ever tried to communicate to someone why you clam up, get angry, freak out a little, feel used instead of loved, or get disgusted when certain things happen? Do any of these feelings rise up when you are asked to do certain things for your partner? These are areas where communication with your spouse is critical for a marriage to be healthy. If your sweetheart does not know why you are pushing away an action, he may assume it is because you do not want *him*. He probably has no idea that whatever the action is could be making your mind, or even just your body, go back to a place that harms you. He views physical intimacy with you in a healthy light, whereas you are still struggling to view it apart from your past.

Listen to these simple words from a woman who had a very hard time with submission for very good reasons:

> *My husband would always want to show his desire for me by coming up behind me and putting his hands on intimate areas of my body. If I did not have my mind on the same things he did at the same moment he did this, I was literally repulsed by the actions. They made me feel that uncomfortable. My body threw up a wall of protection before my mind could catch up to reality. My husband, of course, took this reaction as me not wanting him to touch me. He only saw my rejection of him. If I could have explained to him that my reaction really had nothing to do with him, I think we may still be married. I didn't make the connection until much later that the abuse from my past still made my body feel like I HAD to do the things he wanted, when he wanted, how he wanted, no matter what I wanted—even though my head knew better. The walls I threw up around my body left no room for anyone's desire to blossom—his or mine.*

Many women who have survived abuse find it very difficult to accept a submissive role. Even if they seem to play the part on the outside, life has taught them that they must watch out for themselves. Being under someone's authority can be very challenging because of the last authority they suffered under. A hard life lived can convince anyone that it is darn near impossible to have your own voice if you have to keep bowing your head.

In the Bible, wives are called to submission. This is true. But many people have a misconstrued conception of what submission actually means. Submission does not mean you have to be at someone's beck and call and you never have a say in the matter. Submission is a *voluntary* yielding to another. Husbands and wives are called to very specific roles in God-honoring marriages. Let's take a peek at a few places in Scripture that sum these roles up nicely. We can pick on husbands first, since they aren't here. Turn in your Bible to Ephesians 5:25-30.

When I read these declarations about a godly husband, I wonder if I would ever believe he was real. But that is the hurt speaking. I know that there are many godly men out there, and their character gives me hope.

Verses 25-27 speak of how the man is to love his wife sacrificially. He is to think of her wellbeing before his own. In this way, he is called to a submission of his own, where he voluntarily yields to her at times. His treatment of her as a woman should set her apart from everyone else. This is a truth that is shattered when a man harms a woman physically or mentally. To the man who will follow evil desires, this kind of care for a woman makes no sense whatsoever. Satan encourages him to take whatever he wants from a woman and push the rest of her down in the mud. Satan's lies tell the man that he is her superior and she dare not challenge him. Can you see the difference here?

Verse 28 teaches that the way a husband treats his wife shows the true measure of a man. Verse 29 shows that the husband is to nourish and provide for his love. He is to cherish her. Does this sound like the man who harmed you? _____

Have you ever seen a man treat his wife in this fashion? _____

If so, who, and what did you think about the way he treated her?

_____

_____

_____

Proverbs 5:15-20 unabashedly teaches a man to be "ever captivated by her love." Here, Solomon is teaching his sons that they will find all the intimate fulfillment they will ever need in their wives alone.

The man who honors God with his life will be able to cherish his wife and treat her tenderly. There is no sexual immorality here. No sexual or mental abuse. Submission is a world easier when a person knows that their spouse has their best interests in mind always. When a woman feels this loved, submission is not an issue at all. This is the kind of treatment you should expect from a spouse when you give them the treatment taught in our next Scripture readings. Jump down to verse 33 in Ephesians 5 for a moment. If a man is to love his wife as he loves himself, he *must know* that she respects him. This is critical for a man. Every person shows affection and feels the affections of others differently. We must allow people their healthy uniqueness. You may feel loved when a person writes you a sweet note. A man may feel loved when his woman cooks him a good dinner. Men and women have some basic characteristic needs, and for a man, I have come to realize, respect is at the top of the totem pole. I will delicately also encourage you to never use sex as a weapon against him. That kind of action against your spouse is not what God intended, either. A man's need for this aspect of marriage is as great as your need to feel safe and loved and noticed by him.

Now it is our turn, ladies. We can begin with Proverbs 31:10-31, because this is such a familiar passage for many women. The Scripture here sets a standard for an excellent wife. Though life in modern America is vastly different from what it was in Solomon's day, the focus of this truth is still every bit as valid. The woman's selflessness immensely blesses her family. Mothers and wives have tough, around-the-clock jobs. The Bible recognizes the importance of both roles here.

Now turn to 1 Peter 3 and read through verse 6.

Verses 1 and 2 call for submission and the honorable behavior of a wife, which can show an unbelieving husband who God really is. If you are married to an unbeliever, you must never compromise your faith—especially in the sexual realm. But you must also remember that his choice to follow God is between him and God alone.

Verses 3 and 4 teach that true beauty comes from inside. It should not matter what you wear, what you apply, or how you fix your hair. Those things can be expressions of what you like, but they should never be the focus of your being. Your husband needs to see the person you are inside your heart.

Then, verse 6, I believe, cuts to the heart of the matter. In these words, I see the timelessness of Scripture. Women today carry the same fears in their hearts as women thousands of years ago. This verse encourages women to a voluntary giving up (a submission) of the fears they carry so that they can enjoy life with their husbands. This truth teaches you not to allow fear to cover the beauty inside you. In a way, I think, these words are also a warning against self-fulfilling prophecies. I have seen this happen a time or two—a woman steeped in hurt is in a relationship with a man who truly loves her, but she just won't allow his affections. She keeps the fear of being hurt by him closer than she will ever let him tarry near her heart. She finally pushes him far enough away that her fear is realized when he leaves. She will never admit, in all her self-righteous justifications, that she caused the loss. Bam! She is the victim once again. This is a result of the ties that Satan's deeds bind. The reality of this is absolutely heartbreaking, because this woman will live a continuous cycle of hurt and loss.

Do you push someone away when you think they are getting too close? _____

Have you ever found yourself always assuming the worst before the facts are even presented? _____

Do you realize how destructive this behavior can be? _____
_____

Are you afraid of becoming sexually intimate with a man after the abuse? _____

Learning to trust and open up is terrifying after you have been bashed about. Where are you now in this area? _____
_____

We have been focusing on married life quite a bit, but not all people are called to marriage, and that is perfectly okay. God has not instructed that everyone marry. He did, however, stress the importance of relationships amongst mankind. If you wish to remain single, God has blessings for you, just as He has blessings for those who couple. Your friendships are just as precious to God as the married woman's relationship with her husband. Your healing in the area of sexual abuse is every bit as important as the woman who is going to become sexually active again when she marries (or the woman who is already married). HEALING is what we are after here.

Take a moment to breathe. Here, in the quietness of wherever you are doing your study, rest and know that your life ahead of you can be infinitely lighter without the ties of Satan. He doesn't get to win anymore. He doesn't get to take another thing from you if you say, "Enough is enough already." You have the LORD on your side. Use this study as a tool to fight back. You have the choice.

Sin Resulting from Abuse

A s you walk through today's lesson, do your best to keep an open mind. Maintain a level of grace and a nonjudgmental attitude. Some areas of discussion today really do need to be talked about, but, once again, they may not all pertain to you. Then again, if you feel as if I am stepping on your toes a little too often or too harshly, do not give in to the desire to throw the study out a high window and walk away. Your healing is worth more than that—and please hear me when I say that I have made more mistakes than I ever care to share with anyone. We are also going to get into some of the nitty-gritty, extremely unpleasant-to-discuss sins that stem from sexual abuse. One step at a time, we walk toward freedom. Thankfully, we never walk alone.

RESULTING SIN: WHERE THE SEEDS THAT SATAN PLANTED HAVE GROWN

Because one horrible variation of abuse can happen when one child is abusing another child, we need to clarify this. Somewhere, somehow the child who is abusing another child was introduced to some form of sexual act. Whether they heard about it from a friend, or saw it on television or in a parent's nude magazines or explicit romance novels, they were exposed. When that child was not taught right from wrong, the seed that was planted in their mind grew, and sexual abuse resulted. The point here is that the child *was not* born this way. With that being said, we must recognize two major points.

Not all children who are exposed to sex in any form will become abusers. Many will never speak of it. Some children will tell a person they trust and get the guidance they need. But some will be seriously confused and keep it a secret. Satan's seed will take root and grow. When this confusion is fed by the absence of truth, it can develop into many disturbing things.

The influence that the media has on small minds is immense. We have covered this topic already. Children must be protected from the very visible sex and violence that fill our nation's airwaves, big screens, video games, and young adult novels. Age-appropriate ratings are only effective if they are followed and monitored by parents. Children do not know how they will be influenced by sensuality, love scenes, or nudity in movies. Confusions about what is and is not appropriate sexually come from what a child sees and hears all around them.

I hate that I even need to write the words, but is this where your abuse came from? Was it a childhood friend, a neighborhood kid, a sibling? _____

These are the moments I have to remind myself that God has already won this battle. What Satan is capable of doing to innocent children puts turmoil in my soul the likes of which I cannot explain.

RESULTING SIN: PROMISCUITY

I will let another woman speak on this subject. I will only ask once again for the grace of those who have never dealt with this issue not to judge your sisters who have. Are you familiar with the scene where Jesus calmly said the following to a crowd of angry lawmen? "Let any one of you who is without sin be the first to throw a stone at her" (John 8:7).

Looking back, I can't remember the first time I was forced into sexual activity. As I grew up, I realized that what the men were doing was wrong and that I wanted to get away from them, but I didn't know much else. After I ran away and went to live with another family member, I was left home alone all the time. I was really scared to be alone, especially at night, so I went in search of people to hang out with. The only people I ever found to spend the time with were the teenage boys in the neighborhood. Every boy I met seemed to expect me to have sex with him, so I did. I didn't know what to think about a boy who didn't want that from me, because that is all anybody had wanted from me since I could remember. I can't even remember how many people I have been with. I do know that I really thought I was in love with some of them. That thought makes me sick to my stomach now. I wanted company and to be liked, but I felt used and empty every time it was over. Not one of them ever asked me how I was or even WHO I really was. I knew what all the girls at school thought OF me but no one ever knew ME at all. I was a pretty girl, but so what? Look what it got me. I never even enjoyed what I was doing. It wasn't until after I got married that I even liked being physical with a man. My husband treated me differently. I hate this part of my past. I will never be able to change it, but I have to find a way to move on.

There are so many young girls living their lives like this girl did every day. They are so lost and they have no idea how to stop or where to go for help. People look down on them and cast stones at them because all they see are these actions but never the roots. Have you had any experience yourself, or with someone you know, with this sin resulting from abuse? _____

This is one of the reasons I began to write this study. I know a few young women just like this girl right now. I have to do something to try to help them break out of the cycle and recognize their worth as children of God. God has healed me, mind, body, and soul, in ways that I never thought possible. I cannot keep this gift to myself.

RESULTING SIN: THE CONSTANT VICTIM

Being the victim is not something a person has any control over, but staying the victim is. Staying the victim is often fueled by the intense needs of the hurting. Those intense needs are understandable, but instead of turning to God for healing, the victim tries to manage on their own, looking to themselves and the world for guidance. A world that encourages self-indulgence and self-satisfaction provides ample opportunity for a person to sit in the same spot, churning past and present for a very long time.

When people are unwilling to move past this stage, they begin to settle into the role of the constant victim. Their victimization can be used to gain sympathy and attention. One reason I think people will do this is because they are so desperate for any attention. That desperation, again, is understandable after what they have been through. Drama may feel "normal" to some women because chaos is all they have ever known. They may sometimes make things sound worse than they really were, creating entire worlds of lies to gain this attention. This is so sad, because it plays on the emotions of people who truly care about the victim, and it keeps the victim caught in a snare. The other reason I think people may do this is because they somehow feel like something is owed to them because they have been through so much. I remember feeling at one time that, because so much had been taken from me, I wanted something in return for my sorrows. Have you ever felt anything like this—whether you used it to your advantage or not? _____

_____

One day, I was doing a Bible study, and the reading for the day was in Philippians 3. As I read the words Paul wrote about having a reason to boast about his situation, something clicked. In verses 2-11, Paul says, "If someone else thinks they have reason to put confidence in the flesh, I have more..." What I read in those words was, "If anyone else thinks they have suffered, I have more..." I truly did have a reason to hurt. I had been to hell and back. By the world's standards, I had every reason to be angry and hurt and hate the people who harmed me. After reflecting on those words for a minute, I read on to verse 7: "But whatever were gains to me I now consider loss for the sake of Christ..." I had to stop there a second. Could I? Could I release the satisfaction of the justifications of my suffering and count it as loss? When someone gave me sympathy or showed concern, my suffering was somehow justified because it was acknowledged. I was being seen and heard. Could I give that up when I had lived so long being invisible?

What does verse 8 say? _____

_____

God brought me to a point where He had convinced me that He was real and that He loved me. He showed me that He had plans for my life and that He would always be there to provide me with the strength to walk with Him. In that moment, I felt like He was asking me if I was going to move on. Was knowing Christ, and the love and truth He teaches, worth letting my iron fist release the past?

Until an individual encounters God personally, I do not believe this is possible. There is just too much pain and confusion. We may think we are doing all right, but that is because we have never stepped outside of our lives and felt what it is like to be in God's presence. I hold that truth vividly in my heart, but my words fail in every attempt to convey what knowing God and feeling His love means to me.

YES, I can release the past because *nothing* "compares to the surpassing greatness of knowing Christ Jesus my Lord, for whose sake I have lost all things" (v. 8). Even the things that I once thought benefited me.

When someone gives you a choice, it shows the measure of the love they have for you. God's love for you is great. I pray you are beginning to realize just how great it is. There is no condemnation for the forgiven. Are you willing to let go of the past so that you can know your Savior—so that you can breathe new air and see what life has to offer? _____

_____

_____

_____

_____

Un-forgiveness: The Tie That Binds

No matter what we discuss today, I know full well that forgiveness is one of those things that will happen when, and only when, *you* are ready. I am not going to fire-and-brimstone you to death about this subject. To say "I forgive so-and-so" is one thing. To mean you actually forgive them is another. You will know when you are ready and when you trust God enough to be able to forgive. What I will do today is present some of the guidance that helped me understand what forgiveness was really about. I will also do my best to explain why the cords of un-forgiveness are woven by Satan. He is a crafty thing indeed. With that being said, let's look at some of the things forgiveness is and is not.

One of the things that caused me to hold onto my anger and judgment towards the people who abused me was the idea that they were getting off scot-free. Here I was, dealing with the choices they made, while they happily went on about their lives. Why should they be able to frolic while I drown! Have you ever felt this way?

_____

I do not know if I would have ever looked at things differently if God had not brought a very simple passage to me. Look up Isaiah 57:20, 21. What does this truth proclaim? _____

_____

_____

God has a way of speaking simple truths on deep levels. I do not believe God was trying to tell me to enjoy their turmoil. I think He was trying to get me to see that their lives are a mess. They know no real love or satisfaction. They are blind to all that is good and bright in this world. They have no peace. If someone ever laughs at your pain, or worse yet, wants you to know that your discomfort pleases them, they are sad puppies, my sister. Real love and enjoyment of suffering cannot reside within the same heart. Those two characteristics are antitheses, direct opposites, of one another. After thinking about this a little, I came to the conclusion that I would much rather be me than them.

The other message that really got through to me was the fact that forgiveness is a choice. I am astounded by all the choices Christ-followers get to make. God was even selfless enough to allow Adam to name all of the animals after creation (Gen. 2:19). I do not know why that kindness always warms my heart, but it does. Maybe because it is such a simple gift, the choice to be a part of something God has made. Maybe the act shows me so much of God's character that it keeps pulling me closer. I can only imagine the love of an artist who has created an ultimate masterpiece. He steps back, he takes a breath. He sees that it is good— then, he calls his friend over to allow him to title the piece.

We are presented with another choice early on in Scripture, and it would seem pretty basic also, but life works on us and a layer of fog easily settles atop the path ahead. Deuteronomy 30:11-20 is a beautiful example of one of those foundational truths we talked about the other day. Forgiveness is not preached here, but what God offers every man is clearly defined. What is on the table in verse 15?

_____

_____

We are asked to choose life in the truths proclaimed in the Bible. We are asked to trust that God is bigger than all the things we don't understand and all the things that hurt us. Step back in the Word a couple of verses and read Deuteronomy 29:29: "The _____ things belong to the _____ ..." God asks us to refrain from the temptation of taking matters into our own hands before we seek His guidance. Verse 29 also states "but the things _____ belong to _____ ..." We have to trust that He will reveal to us what we need to know when we need to know it. I know that waiting is a difficult pastime. I have never been proficient at the sport, and less-than-rarely do I enjoy that game. God does not ask us to wait because He likes to see us struggle. He asks us to wait because it is in the waiting that we most often commune with Him. He asks us to wait so that we will not miss what He has planned for us. Sometimes, in our haste to take action, we can make grave mistakes. To forgive takes great patience. To be unforgiving is swift action. Read these haunting words from a woman who has learned to wait:

> *The man who raped me took his own life in an empty motel room with a long-barreled shotgun. I will confess that I had thought of being the one to pull that trigger a few times. He threatened my life so regularly I felt that I would eventually have to take his in order to keep mine. He left a note. The police said one of the lines read, "I'm sorry for the things I've done." He came to a point where he realized the gravity of his actions, and it was too much for him to bear. I get no satisfaction out of his death, only a peace in knowing that he will never hurt me again. I would like to think that if he had come to a point of real change and asked my forgiveness, I would have released him. I would like to think that I would have moved out of the way and allowed God to work on his heart without being a constant blaming reminder of his greatest mistakes. I would like to think I could have been capable of helping change someone's life, but I will never know because he chose death.*

It has never been easy for me to even attempt to look at the abuser as a person, but somehow this woman's story got me to pause. He could not forgive himself for what he had done. He had no trust in God to redeem him; thus, Satan won his life. The harshly woven cords of un-forgiveness became a noose, or in this case a long-barreled shotgun. As vile as I believe these abusers are, I *must* begin to see them as lost. Vile still, and with evil inside them that I want no part of, but lost people. I will not proclaim that I will readily accept their conversions when I hear about them, but if *anyone* were going to truly change, I would not want to be in their way. A changed person means less pain in the world, amongst other things.

When you choose to forgive, you choose life. More often than not, your life will not be the only life that is affected. To forgive does not mean to say that what that person did was okay. You are not giving them permission to do the deed again. Forgiving an offense doesn't mean you are weak. You are simply making a choice to separate yourself from the deed that wronged you. You are displaying your trust in God that He will take care of the offense and the offender. You have the choice to lay that burden down at the foot of the cross and step into the freedom being offered. What matters more to you: the thing you will never be able to change, or the future you have waiting for you?

What does Deuteronomy 30:17, 18 promise if you choose to turn away? _____

Hasn't there been enough destruction in your life? Verses 19 and 20 warn that holding the cords of un-forgiveness will hinder your ability to hear God's voice. I starkly remember what my life was like before I began learning about God. I heard so many things in my mind. I heard the laughter of the men who harmed me and the threats they made. I heard the angry yelling of so-and-so. I heard the judgment of others. I heard the whispers of the strangers who said, "Look at her; she will never be anybody worth anything." I do not hear these things anymore. I do not always hear God's voice, but I can tell you one thing: I never want to miss hearing His voice because His voice cuts through all those other voices.

How do you see the people/person who harmed you? Do you see them as people or "as things?" _____

_____

What thoughts do you have in your mind about forgiveness right now? _____

_____

We are almost there my friend.
LORD, help us complete this work, I pray. Amen.

Week 7

Take Back Your Gardens

God's Promise: You are forgiven. You are clean, loved, and beautiful. You can be free!

Do you believe this? _____

Why? Why not? _____

_____

_____

Satan's Lie: You'll never change. You're not forgiven. You are forever damaged goods.

Do you believe this? _____

Why? Why not? _____

_____

_____

Who God Created You to Be. You, Specifically.

Here we are: week seven. I am so very thankful that you have continued on with this work. I am praying that by now you have begun to look at yourself and the abuse you survived a little differently. You have dug around in some of the darkest reaches of your past, and I am praying that you are a stronger woman for it today. We are going to take an intense look at that woman this week. We do not want to leave one stone unturned on this quest. I know that what we go through in life does not completely leave us until death, but you and I and our sisters are still here. Today is a gift to you from the Creator of life. Do not allow Satan to take another thing from you! A healed woman is a conundrum to evil, because darkness thinks, and so does most of the world, that we should all end up like Tamar from week three: desolate.

Desolate ... no, I don't think so my dear sister. I saw a shadow of a woman one time that absolutely broke me down. Looking at her was like looking at an abandoned house. You know the kind of "abandoned" I am talking about: That sort of house where the weeds have encroached to the point that the yard blends in with the natural vegetation of the land. The one where the windows are broken out and the bleak emptiness of the interior shows through. There was no longer the vibrancy of a well tended, spirited woman; there was only the shadow of her former self. She was utterly desolate. How about we not accept desolation? Let's dig deeper and draw closer to God. Let's shut evil attacks down!

If, in the past, you have believed Satan's lies, maybe today will be the day you stop listening to them. Maybe you will finally realize what you *are not* and start living for what you *are*. Today, we will look at two Scripture segments that deal with that very idea. We have only a handful of steps left to take together. Let us begin the close of our study.

Turn with me to Genesis 32. Within these pages, we will encounter Jacob once again. He has had an interesting journey so far, but his life is about to completely change. For those of you unfamiliar with Jacob, he was born the twin of Esau, son of Isaac and Rebekah. Jacob stole Esau's birthright and inheritance by carrying out a scheme of great deception (Gen. 25, 27). Then, Jacob had to get out of Dodge pretty quickly because Esau wished to have his brother's head for said deception. God had to step in and intervene in Jacob's life because He had other plans for this Patriarch. However, before those plans could be realized, Jacob had to discover *who he was not*.

In Genesis 32:22-30, God orchestrates some good, old-fashioned "alone time" for Jacob. Sometimes the distractions in our lives are so loud we may not be able to hear God clearly until we are alone with Him. I encourage you to find a spot in your home, or wherever you feel best, and get alone with God in your deep prayers. Get somewhere away from distractions where you can really think, and listen. Jacob was a bit hardheaded, so he required a more aggressive interruption than that calm, still whisper so often spoken by the Lord. What happens to Jacob in verse 24? _____

_____

Then, in verse 25? _____

_____

The word "overpower" in verse 25 means that Jacob would not stop wrestling with "the man." If Jacob were to truly overpower the man, one touch from the man to Jacob's hip socket would not have been enough to disable Jacob. Even still, Jacob would not release the man. Jacob had encountered something far greater than himself in the quiet of the night, and he wanted a blessing from it (v. 26). So, in the next breath, I believe "the man" held Jacob's full attention, and He asked the only question that mattered in that pivotal moment in Jacob's life. What does the man ask Jacob in verse 27? _____

_____

The man was not just asking for Jacob's name; a far more important question was on the table. He was really asking Jacob, "*Who* are you?" The children of that era were christened not with a name, but with an identity, much like our actions can seem to define who we are to people watching us. Jacob's name meant "deceiver," and in that moment of struggle, he was forced to look at himself and his life and admit *who* he was. In no way could Jacob deny that he had lived up to his name, so he answered with the truth. That honesty of self-reflection and unrelenting desire for a blessing were ingredients one and two that brought on Jacob's change. The third part of that soul-shifting mix was Jacob's undeniable encounter with God. Hold this thought for a breath and look a few lines further.

What happens in verse 28? _____

_____

_____

God, for that is who "the man" really was, helps Jacob see who he is not in order that he may move forward with who he is growing to be: *Israel.* "Israel" means "he struggles or persists *with* God." Israel lived his life with God where Jacob did not. Israel was able to acknowledge his mistakes, receive grace to make peace with them, and move forward from his past. What is the point of grace if not to allow us to move forward?

Verse 29 holds something very interesting, a truth I think we should not overlook. Picture the scene with me. Jacob stands there as the darkness of night is receding around him and the darkness of his old life is receding within him. He seems a little overwhelmed. He has received a blessing that promises a security he has never known. He looks in wonder at the "man" before him and asks for

His name. It sounds like Jacob is saying, "Could you help me put my finger on what just happened here?" How does God answer Jacob in verse 29? _____

_____

It seems to me that God is saying to Jacob, "Why is it that you cannot see who *I* am?"

There had been so many things clouding Jacob's vision. Isn't the same true with us today? God is literally all around us, but the struggles and the human desires we carry can overshadow His presence. I think God had shown Himself to Jacob so many times that Jacob really *should have* been able to recognize Him, and right here God is asking Jacob why he still can't. What is in the way? Is there still something in your way? _____

_____

When Israel was close to death, he remembered what the Lord had taught him on that day. Turn to Genesis 48:15, 16 and read Israel's words of reflection. The New American Standard renders verse 16 like this: "The angel who has redeemed me from all evil ..." Redemption was the goal all along, and redemption cannot happen apart from recognition and acceptance of the Maker.

The other account we will look at today really resonated in my heart the first time I read it. This story brings us a man who was named "sorrow" by his mother, but he did not allow her choices to taint who he would become. Turn to 1 Chronicles 4:9, 10. Even though his name meant sorrow, how is Jabez described? _____

_____

_____

Why do you think that is? Take another peek at verse 10 if you need a hint. _____

_____

_____

Jabez was born into the effects of another's choices. He had no say in the matter. Why would a person ever name their child "sorrow"?

(The confusing depths of pain, that's why.) Jabez did not want to accept this identity, but he knew that he could not "make" himself greater, so he asked for a blessing, just like Jacob did when he found the One who was stronger than anything he had ever encountered. Where Israel needed a little help to realize who he was not, Jabez clearly understood that the key to victory was a prayer and some faith. Israel could have believed that shadowed lie that taunts "you will never change." Jabez could have believed that he was forever tainted goods because of somebody else's confusion. But these two men had encounters with God that silenced those cruel lies.

Have you ever worried that you would follow in the footsteps of the parent that harmed you? _____

_____

This is not an uncommon fear, if you have it, but you do not need to worry that you will be anything like them. They made their choices, and you will make yours. You are not damaged goods. Nor are you doomed to have any of the same tendencies. Some of you may not need to hear that, but some of our sisters do.

Have you ever been so angry at someone for not treating you the way they should that you became frustrated to the point that things just did not make any sense? How can you love fully, completely, when they never loved you? How can you vow to die before you ever let someone hurt your child or loved one, and they willingly stepped out of the way and left you vulnerable? Have you ever wondered how they could betray you, lie to you, laugh when you hurt? No need to tone down your answer, just say what you feel. _____

_____

_____

I held very few things close to me as a child. All that I loved was either taken or ridiculed. I rarely knew kindness, and I saw flickers of love even less. However, one idea was planted in my head that was somehow never shaken, and it had come from a children's story that I read in school. There was this one passage in the book that caught my little heart and held on tight: A velveteen rabbit was asking a skin horse what it meant to be real. The skin horse told the rabbit, "When a child loves you, really loves you, *then* you become real." (I am paraphrasing a bit here.)

Then, the rabbit asks: "Does it hurt?"

And the wise skin horse answers: "When you are real, you don't mind being hurt. It doesn't happen all at once. You *become*. It can take a long time. That's why it doesn't happen to people who break easily, or have sharp edges, or have to be carefully kept." Then, he tells the rabbit that it doesn't matter what you look like when you are real, because once you are real, you can't be ugly. Then the rabbit longs to become real. To know what it feels like.[1]

That passage in that little torn-up book kept coming back to me every time someone called me ugly, every time someone hit me and then laughed at my suffering. Those people were not *real* in my mind. They knew nothing about love or kindness. They had "sharp edges," so to speak. This passage kept saying to me to be strong, to never break, because one day *I* would be real. What separates me from the people who abused me is the simple fact that somehow I understood that I was going to know love. First John 4:19 states, "We love because He first loved us."

Understanding God's love is so much like this story. Sometimes it hurts because we do not understand what God knows. Sometimes long years pass before anything makes sense. But then, when we finally feel loved, really loved, by God, it doesn't matter that things hurt or what we look like, because nothing God loves is ugly, if it feels and returns His love. I am "real." He loves me, and that is why I am able to love where someone else was only able to harm. Somehow, I always knew that truth; God just used a little faded book to help me hang onto it before I could hear His voice. When I wonder why the people in my life made the choices that they did, I try to remember that the key to loving is being loved.[2]

Does this make any sense to you? _____

_____

_____

When you look at yourself in the mirror, who do you see? Do you see a woman still bound and defined by her mistakes? Do you see the abuse? Or maybe—with all my heart I pray—do you see grace? Do you see a path to move forward? _____

_____

_____

_____

_____

_____

I want to close today's lesson with the lyrics to one of my favorite songs.

At the foot of the cross; Where grace and suffering meet
You have shown me Your love; Through the judgment You
received

And You've won my heart
Yes You've won my heart
Now I can

Trade these ashes in for beauty;
And wear forgiveness like a crown
Coming to kiss the feet of mercy; I lay every burden down
At the foot of the cross

At the foot of the cross; Where I am made complete
You have given me life; Through the death You bore for me

Lord, I am praying for the day we can all sing this song of the redeemed.

B. M. D. A. G. C. L. D. B. M. K. S. M. P. D. D. R. B. T. A. H. L. E. M. T. E. M. L. C.

You may be wondering what on earth the title of today's lesson means. The question is not what, but who. Those are the first letters of the first names of the girls and the women that I know today, not just in all my life but today, who have suffered from sexual abuse. To protect their privacy, I will leave them as letters on this page, but I want them to know that this work was written for them. This work is also for you. This work that took me thirty-some-odd years to drag my beaten, scarred, and tired body through is for all of the women who have ever suffered from sexual abuse. For every time I asked, "WHY is this happening to me?" For every time the confusion of my mind weighed too heavily. For every "WHY? WHY?? OH MY GOODNESS, WHY?"—this is why.

When God began to heal me, I still asked WHY! When I grew stronger and closer to Him, I still asked WHY! I believe, without a doubt, that this work for you is one of the main reasons why. If God allowed me to suffer in order that one day He could use what He taught me as a tool to reach out to you, then I am ever grateful. I NEVER thought those words would come out of my mouth connected to *this* subject matter, but I am. And I know that another reason why is that through all this, I have come to know my God in an undeniably real way.

The first flames of this work were sparked years ago in my mind when I read Luke 22:31, 32. What is going on in these two verses?

_____

_____

_____

Bluntly put, Satan asks for permission to put Simon Peter through hell. This, again, affirmed the theology that all things pass through God's hands before they ever touch us. That idea made me ask WHY again.

What does Jesus promise to do for Simon? _____

_____

That truth gave me great comfort ... but I still asked WHY.

Then, verse 32 hit home, and it all began to make sense. What are we meant to do after we "turn back?" _____

_____

Because of God's gift of free will, there will be evil in this world until the end of days. The same evil lives here now that lived here when Jesus prayed for Simon to overcome. God knows that when we encounter that evil, we may turn from Him in our pain and confusion. That is why He Himself prays for our strength. Some of us will grab hold of that power and use the strength to gain healing and fight for others. Some people will never know His love, and they will be lost forever; and Satan will have won.

Did you ever turn away in your pain? _____

_____

Did you ever mock the thought of a "loving God?" _____

_____

Does it ever cross your mind that there may be some reason for all that has come to pass? _____

No one ever wants to be the one who suffers so that God may shine through their lives. I have never heard anyone say, "Pick me! Pick me to be devastated for Your sake, my Lord!" I am guessing you didn't. I know that I sure didn't. Joseph didn't either. Do you know Joseph's story? Betrayed and abandoned by his brothers, because of their jealousy, left alone to die, then sold alone into slavery, wrongfully imprisoned for another's anger, wondering for years WHY these things happened to him. One day, he got his answer— and he shared it with the very ones who caused his suffering. Turn with me to look at one of the greatest moments of truth and grace in the Old Testament, Genesis 50:15-21.

Who is coming to see Joseph in this passage? _____

_____

Why are they afraid to see their brother? _____

_____

The brothers sent a plea for forgiveness to the one they had seriously harmed. They had good reason to be shaking in their sandals, and Joseph had every reason to hate them. Joseph was now so powerful in the land that he could have exerted vengeance upon those men and been completely justified. But instead, he ... wept. Instead, he held fast to the knowledge that he was not God. Joseph had lived enough life to understand that not one breath is wasted. What does he tell his brothers in verse 20? _____

_____

_____

Someone may have intended to hurt you, but God has other plans for that moment of your life. The people who suffer in this world need to see the people who have overcome. In that way, lives take one step closer to being saved with the pain you were dealt.

Read about how this woman handled a "Joseph moment":

> One afternoon, my mother had come to visit and we were driving into town for some errand or another. Our visits always bordered on the tense side of obligation to begin with, so I was ready to get things done and head home. At some point during the drive, we were stopped at a traffic light and she casually said to me, "You know, I never really meant to hurt

you." I heard those words and that old familiar aggression rose up inside me fast and hard. The images began playing like a silent, horror-movie slide show. Me, small, young, cowering under her yells. Me, abandoned in a hospital, broken arm, headed for surgery. Me, left in the care of people she KNEW were harming me. Me, begging her to please come get me before I was harmed again. Me, at an utter emotional loss as she stole my paychecks and, in a very "in your face" kind of way, spent them on herself. Me, Me, Me. For a few awkward minutes, the images just kept coming. She spoke these very causal, passive "I never meant to hurt you" words to make herself feel better at my expense, as always. She either couldn't see, or refused to see, how they affected me. I wanted to throw twenty-eight years of heartache in her face and MAKE her see, but something stopped me. Something told me that that kind of reaction would never change anything. It would only keep the cycle going, and maybe my story was intended for something else.

God will never agree to allow you to travel a bridge He cannot and will not help you cross. The testimony that is your life can be used to give hope to another who has no hope. You may never be called to write a Bible study or speak in front of a crowd. You may never be asked to publicly share a single word of what you have gone through, but the victory in your life will not be overlooked. Someone who knows you, someone who has glimpsed the suffering in your life, will one day see the healing, and that could be all the testimony they will ever receive. But I will tell you this: your testimony will not be wasted. It will be used to bring light into the darkness of this world. Your story, your victory, could be a lifeline to a person who is dangling over a pit of lava. You are one less trophy Satan gets to gloat over. I will never forget the first time someone told me that my story gave her the courage to get out of bed on a day she wanted to never get up again. She only knew a little bit of my history, but she knew a lot about who I am today.

If you go back to the book of Jude and read verses 20-24, you will find a charge. First, there is a call to "build yourselves up" in your faith. Then, to keep yourself in God's love. And, finally, to "be _____ to those who _____;" and to "_____ others from the _____ and _____ them ..." (v. 22, 23). Please do not mistake this for a call to be someone's savior. Only One holds that title. We do not have the ability to save anyone's soul, and thank goodness we don't. That is not a burden we could ever bear, but God does clearly direct His people to be active in His work.

By the grace of God I am what I am, and His grace to me was not without effect (1 Cor. 15:10). I know that I am alive today because of the grace of God. If my life can bring another person hope, then I will say Amen! Again, and again, Amen!

Temptations and Faith

One thing you can be absolutely certain of is the fact that once you begin healing, you will begin facing a whole new breed of temptations. You see, you have gained some hard-won ground, and Satan will want to take that from you. But this is your victory, so let's look at a few ways to combat temptation when it does come.

I think the first thing that needs to be understood about temptation is that it does not come from God. Look up James 1:13-15 and write out what verse 13 says: _____

_____

_____

There seems to be a common misconception camping around this truth, so let's think about it for a second. Besides the fact that the Word clearly states temptation does not come from God, what can temptation lead to? _____ When we *give in* to temptation, sin follows. Now, of course, I am not talking about being tempted by your sweet tooth to eat a candy bar, so long as you do not have an eating disorder (eating disorders are not to be taken lightly and I believe the root of those issues lies in a struggle for control). These temptations will be of the variety that will cause you to choose between following God or turning from His truth. They will appear harmless at first—and very attractive. They will also probably be centered around some deep desire or need you have.

Some examples of temptations would be: Do I release my anger on so-and-so for being a jerk to me, so I can sting them back and feel better? Do I flirt with so-and-so to feel good? Do I quietly highlight someone else's mistakes at work so I can step up the ladder? Do I comfort a married male coworker after his hard day? Do I continually put off meeting with other believers or reading Scripture because I am tired and just don't want to have to be another place on time? You get the idea. Simply understand that God will *never* lead you into sin. That would be counterproductive to His entire message. God will surely test His children, but never tempt them.

When God tests a person, it is for the purpose of developing authentic character and building faith. Look up Proverbs 27:21. Sometimes, receiving praise is a test. We may need a quick survey to see where our hearts lie. For example, does praise feed a little hungry monster inside you? Or, when receiving praise, do you smile and thank the Lord for giving you whatever talent you have?

Have you ever felt like your faith was being tested? When? How? _____

_____

_____

Often, a test is more for us to see what we are capable of than anything else. Just try to remember that a test is always for the purpose of building your character and drawing you closer to God.

Perhaps the next thing we should talk about is the company you keep. Some people believe that when you give your life to God, you must turn away from everyone you know who is not a believer. Once again, this would be counterproductive to the message Christ brought into the world. (Mark 16:15: "Go into all the world and preach the gospel to all creation.") How are you supposed to show someone God's love and character if you exclude them from your life or turn a polished little nose up at them? Have you ever seen a churchgoing Christian act like they were better than someone who looks a little rough around the edges? _____

_____

_____

I would suggest to you that that person might not be paying much attention while they are at church. The only time you should end a relationship is if the relationship is destructive in some way.

We definitely need to spend a little time on learning how to resist temptation. Satan will tempt you relentlessly, and I find no better method of defense than the one Jesus shows to us in the 22nd chapter of Luke. I cannot imagine how powerful this night was in all of time. Yet still, Christ teaches through His valley of death. What is going on in Luke 22:39-46? _____

_____

_____

First of all, please note that Christ did not change His routine while He dealt with this struggle. Second, please note that Christ did not separate Himself from His support group. Finally, I want to draw your attention to what Christ says in verse 46. What does He say to the disciples here? _____

_____

_____

Why do you think resting and being alone would pull a person into temptation? _____

_____

_____

Did you notice that the disciples were exhausted? We can make some of our worst mistakes due to exhaustion. Have you ever said something you shouldn't have said when you were too tired or stressed to filter your words first? Have you ever given in to an addiction or fallen to a weakness when you were stretched too thin to be strong any longer? I have, and it was ugly.

I think Christ is teaching us that faith and obedience to that faith are *diligent pursuits*. Doing nothing would be much easier than standing your ground or hitting your knees in prayer. But doing nothing in the face of adversity leads to defeat. God will not simply take the temptation away from you, because some action is required on our parts. If our Father took every challenge from us before we had to flex some muscle to get through the situation, we would never grow to learn anything. We would not be held to any standards, or draw closer to Him. We would not have *choice*.

I think about the void depression pulls a person into—how they feel so completely empty, lost and sometimes even unable to physically move. Movement brings breath into tired lungs. Breath brings life. God breathed life into us when we were created. I think Christ is saying to inhale the breath of God! When He says in verse 46, "Get up and _____ ..." He is encouraging your diligent pursuit of faith. May you find strength in the fact that "The prayer of a righteous person is powerful and effective" (Jam. 5:16).

That beautiful truth brings us to our next point. 1 Corinthians 10:13 is a promise that I have had to read countless times over. What does this word literally say? _____

_____

_____

Now, after you ponder this a minute, kindly tell me what this word can mean to *your* life. _____

_____

_____

God does not wish for you to fall. You will not be forced to endure something that will crush you, even though you may feel like that is the case. At every step, He is there beside us with the way out. (Even if you do succumb to temptation, because no one is perfect, God is still available to you when you are ready to make different choices.) There is *always* another choice. The choices may not always be easy, but temptation is never only a dead-end road. I gravely wonder how many times in my life I could have been spared a vast amount of heartache if I had merely turned my head towards Him. One of my favorite people in the whole world has this annoying saying that is so true (hence the annoyance): "Those who can't listen must feel."

Another thing to keep in mind when dealing with temptation is Ephesians 6:10-18. What threat do we face in verse 16? _____

_____

_____

_____

What does verse 11 say those flaming arrows are a part of?

_____

_____

_____

That word "scheme" denotes a methodical planned-out attack. It helps me to remember that there are bigger forces at work than just me and my sinful desires. There is a battle taking place which goes far beyond the realms of "flesh and blood." Evil is powerful, yes, but so is faith! Your faith is your connection to the One who is stronger than the evil in this world. Without faith, you cannot know God at all (Heb. 11:6). Ephesians 6 gives mighty instruction on how to arm yourself against temptation. The moment you begin to heal from all the ways evil has affected your life, temptation will abound. Satan is going to come at us with both barrels loaded—never be passive or doubtful about that—and he always seems to have seven bullets in his six-shooter gun. His schemes will come in all shapes and disguises. Flaming arrows will set sail to pierce your heart, body, and mind. Never forget that you have protection available just a breath away. You are precious cargo, my sister.

When you are tempted to think that everyone will be like someone from your past, remember this lesson. When you are tempted to throw in the towel and give up, remember the strength promised to you in the Scriptures. When you are presented with the opportunity to dabble in your addictions or your weaknesses, or even your self-preserving solitude, REMEMBER who is attacking you, again! Remember that at some point, you will doubt; at some point, you will suffer again. But for the love of all that is good and holy in this world, remember the power of your faith!

What are your most challenging temptations? _____

_____

_____

_____

_____

How do you normally combat those things when they flare? ___

_____

_____

_____

_____

_____

_____

Do you understand the difference between being tested by God and being tempted by Satan? _____

_____

_____

_____

_____

_____

_____

_____

_____

_____

_____

Gardens Are for Flowers, Not Weeds

There is this poem I read a few months ago that struck me as a deep, emotional truth from the heart of any woman who has ever suffered abuse. The woman in the poem is a slave from the pre-Civil War South. The lines that stood out the most read: "My Maker says I am a garden / full of secrets and beauty and soul ... My master says they are naught but weeds ..." Her Maker was the LORD. Her master was Satan and his cunning followers.

Have the "weeds" of abuse so overgrown your heart and mind that your beauty is hidden and your secrets are silent? Are those "weeds" chains that attempt to keep your soul from ever taking flight? The goal of the Evil One is to make you believe that everything good and lovely inside you has been ripped out of that beautiful garden. What he and God both know is that he may only attempt to cover the life in your garden so fully that flowers will never be seen. He cannot completely take from you what God has created inside you, but he can plant some devastating weeds. (If you have ever tried to maintain a Texas lawn then you are getting a clear analogy, I'm sure!)

I came across another story from a girl who had physical representations of those "weeds." For a very long time, she was unable to look at anything else.

Fourteen found me scarred from the abuse I had suffered, and homeless. I walked the streets of a state that ended my travels only because it was bordered by an ocean. I would have run farther if I could. I was sitting there one day, alone and hungry, wondering what in the world I was going to do for shelter that night, when some flashes of light caught my eye. There, in the middle of the shopping area I was haunting, was a group of models doing a photo shoot. It was a bit surreal, watching those perfect figures strut and pose like they did not have a care in the world. They were very beautiful with their perfect skin and pretty clothes. I was sure they weren't hungry or looking for a place to sleep. I was watching them when one of the photographers caught my stare. He looked at me for a minute and then began to walk over to me. I didn't know what to do, so I sat there like a statue. When he got to me, he began talking to me while he intently looked me over. His eyes more often rested on my many scars than on my eyes. I didn't blame him, though. I rarely, if ever, saw past them myself. When he walked away, I was not surprised. For most of my life, I thought those scars defined me. The day I realized that beauty was not a physical thing was the day I began to look at myself differently. I began to understand that physical beauty and self-worth were not synonymous. Someone had invited me to church, and even though I was leery about going, I went. It took a while, but I learned what God saw when He looked at me. He didn't see scars. He didn't want me to see scars either. It took encountering Christ to show me that I was more than the scars on my body.

This girl had literal scars that covered her like a blanket and stole her sight. Many of us do, as well. We are also marked by emotional scars that have the same power to steal our focus and cover our beauty. We can't change the past, but we can choose to set our minds on other things. I love how Colossians 3:2 calls us to "Set your minds on things above, not on earthly things," so how about looking at some of those "things above" in today's lesson. Can I ask you another serious question? Have you ever wondered what you have beyond the life the abuse gave you? _____

_____

_____

It's sort of a "What else is there?" question. I know that, when I began peeling off those terrible layers life had painted on me, I had to discover who I was in many ways. I got to discover what *I* liked to do. I found out how *I* liked to spend my time and who *I* liked to be around. I got to learn how *I*, outside of abuse, would deal with different situations that came and went. I remember thinking, one time, how free I felt without the constant doom-and-gloom feelings. I think I began to look at other lighter, more hopeful options, because I finally knew I could choose those without that old, hateful "When is the other shoe going to drop?" fear.

Have you ever experienced the distracting power of a good laugh? Laughter has a way of cutting through grief or weariness, if only for a moment. Humor definitely has the ability to saw through tension. The truth in Colossians 3:2 has the same principle. Love destroys fear, kindness overrides rude character, truth exposes lies, faith pushes temptation away, prayer breeches the walls of loneliness because it draws you closer to God. If you find yourself with a negative or harmful thought in your head that you don't want to think about anymore, just set your mind on things above. Invite some of God's light in. Philippians 4:8, 9 encourages us to think about "whatever is _____, whatever is _____, whatever is _____, whatever is _____, whatever is _____, whatever is _____—if anything is _____ or _____—think about such things." If we do this, then what are we guaranteed to have with us (v. 9)? _____

_____

Have you had enough destruction? Wouldn't you like a little peace?

If you skip back up the page to Philippians 4:6, we are also encouraged to pray about everything. If you need wisdom or physical strength, pray for it. If you need help getting over something, pray about that, too. If you just want to have a good day or a restful night's sleep, you guessed it! You can pray about that, too. Please pray for the people you know and love. Make sure, though, that when you do pray, your motives are correct (Jam. 4:3) so that you may see many more answered prayers. You will not receive what you ask for at all, if your motives for the request do not honor the Giver. Understand that nothing is hidden from God. He sees even the secret things of the heart, and just as He will not tempt you, He will not give you something that will pull you away from Him.

Something my pastor challenged our congregation to do a few years ago was to find out what our unique gifts were. Instead of coveting another's talent, he encouraged us to ask God to reveal our own talents. (Yes, you have a talent.) One of the passages he focused on was 1 Corinthians 12. Look at verses 4-6, then verses 12-20. Growing up, did anyone ever focus on what you were good at? ____

_____

Do you have a talent of some sort? _____

_____

If you could set a goal towards any ability, what would you like to be able to do? _____

_____

The point here is to know that you have a unique place in the body of Christ. You have gifts given to you from God, specifically designed for you individually, and for your family universally. You may be able to sing, or write, or cook, or pray with hurting people, or listen like no other, or organize, or run a computer program, a sound booth, a pumpkin patch. You may have a talent in caring for animals, or sick people, or children. Find out what you do best, and set your mind on it. You have got to fill your life with new, healthy things. You may feel like you have nothing to offer, and no time to offer it, even if you did have something. This is a great deception, for you have much to offer. What gifts you have is not the issue—your focus and belief in yourself is. Set aside a piece of time to look at the big picture, and then move forward with your life. This might be a good time to examine your daily routine. Is there something unhealthy you could take off your plate, or maybe something you could spend a little less time on?

Lord, I pray that we will begin to take a little time to discover what our secrets are. You have created in each of us a beautiful, special, talented woman. You have watered us with strength and love from Your Spirit. I pray for my sisters and for myself that when we feel overwhelmed, we will remember Your promises. I pray that Your truth will speak louder than our past. Lord, protect us from those who will attempt to tear us down. Help us to focus on all the good You have given to us. Help us to know You, LORD; in the name of Christ. Amen.

Is there something on your plate that you may have pushed over to the edge and not focused on a little too often, like a husband, or a relationship with a child, or a project you really need to finish?

_____

_____

_____

What are some ways that you can "pull them back closer to the center," so to speak? _____

_____

_____

_____

_____

_____

_____

_____

_____

Emmanuel: God with Us

My sisters, there were days I thought we would never reach this page. I cannot tell you what this journey has given me. I am honored that I have had the chance to fight back against some of the evil in this world with the truth God has shown me. I wish that I could rejoice in every step of your healing with you face-to-face! I have very little to write today—all the hard work has been done these past seven weeks. I do, however, have some searching questions for you. (Big shocker there, huh?) I also have some last encouragements for you, and then it is up to you where you wish to go from here.

Take encouragement in the truth that God gave you a spirit of strength. For the last time in our study, let us dig into the Word of God for guidance. First turn to 2 Timothy 1:7. When God created you, what did He weave into your spirit? _____

_____

Reach inside and allow this truth to speak to you when you worry that things will never be different. There are so many people who wish to believe in an "ask and you shall receive anything you want, everyone will prosper, roses and pretty pictures" gospel, but, my sister, that is not real life, and it certainly is not the gospel. Life is going to bring challenges, and everyone will not find wealth and good health and long life here on earth. To believe such things is to live in a fairytale world created by an unwillingness to deal with trouble when it comes. You have everything you need to overcome anything you encounter. You have a powerful spirit with a great ability to love, and you have a God who will never leave you. He will speak truth into your life if you listen.

When someone or something tries to tell you that God is not real, reflect on all you have seen and learned. Pray for God to reveal Himself to you. Look around at the marvels of this earth and sky. Surrender to the love you hold in your heart and *know* where that love came from.

When someone or something tries to get you to believe that you made the abuse up, or that it was all you fault, do not listen! Turn to God. Ask for the truth in ALL situations to be revealed to you. Do not allow Satan to whisper confusion into your mind. Stand firm in your freedom.

When you are tempted to take judgment into your own hands, remember that all life belongs to God. You bring nothing into this world, nor did you create yourself. You have no idea what tomorrow will hold. God created life, and will judge every single soul accordingly. What if today is all you get? Don't worry about the things you cannot change. Focus instead on what God has filled your life with. There is still joy all around to be had every single day.

Do not listen when you are tempted to believe that you do not matter. You matter! Just because someone chose to harm you doesn't mean they can take your worth. Throw off their sin and reopen your heart. There is so much freedom in being able to trust someone. Remember that relationships without trust are doomed to fail. Humans are bent towards acceptance. Mistrust screams, "You are not accepted!" and that will kill a relationship stone-cold.

Know beyond a shadow of a doubt that when God looks at you, He sees straight into the soul of who He created. He sees everything He made you to be and *that* is who He speaks to when He speaks to you. You have never been nothing, for you are everything to God.

When you get hurt, do not allow the pain to convince you that everyone is the same and you will never be truly loved. There are so many good people in this world, but they, too, will make mistakes—

just as you will make mistakes. But love covers mistakes. Allow the people in your life to be human. It is simply unfair to hold someone to a standard that no one can obtain.

When you turn the TV on, open a book, or go to a movie, be mindful of the true meaning of physical intimacy. You do not need to live in a hole, but you will need to be diligent about purity. Remember that this battle is much more easily won when you are standing close to your Lord. Remember that your woman-ness is a gift you alone are allowed to give to a man in love. And remember that his desire for that woman in you is God-given desire, not to be feared, not to be mistrusted.

And if you take only one thing from this study, let it be the knowledge that God is with you wherever you go. He is Emmanuel, God with us.

Now it is your turn. Just two questions for our conclusion:

1. Was there an aspect of the abuse you suffered that was not covered in this study? _____

_____

_____

_____

_____

_____

What questions do you have, or what issues are you still struggling with, due to that specific aspect? _____

_____

_____

_____

_____

_____

2. Was there a particular day's lesson or weekly topic that really helped you deal with the abuse? _____

_____

_____

_____

_____

_____

_____

Thank you for the time you spent in this study. Thank you for giving God a chance to combat the evil that has been forced into your life. He rejoices over you with singing. He delights in your healing. As do I, my sister. As do I. Don't ever give up. You have a life to live and love to know.

May The LORD bless you and keep you;
The LORD make His face shine on you
And be gracious to you;
The LORD turn His face toward you
And give you peace.

Numbers 6:24-26

If your law had not been my delight,
Then I would have perished in my affliction.
I will never forget your precepts,
For by them you have revived me.
I am Yours, save me.

Psalm 119:92-94

Study Outline

WEEK 1: IS HE REAL? AND IF SO...

God's Promise: That He will reveal Himself to you. That He wants a personal relationship with you.

Satan's Lie: God is not real. God is not the only God. God is not powerful. God will not talk to you.

Day 1: Plans? What Plans?
Day 2: Why Does He Let These Things Happen?
Day 3: Where Was He When...!
Day 4: His Ways Are Higher
Day 5: Why Was I Made?

WEEK 2: SOMETIMES YOU HAVE TO GO BACK

God's Promise: The truth will set you free. (John 8:32)

Satan's Lie: You made it up. It's your fault.

Day 1: Look Straight at It...
Day 2: Issues: Anger
Day 3: A Serious Lack of Peace: More Issues
Day 4: Right, Wrong, and Still Gray
Day 5: A Worthy Intercessor

WEEK 3: NOT A DESOLATE WOMAN!

God's Promise: He will search for you, He will bind you up. (Ezk. 34:16) He will give you NEW strength. (Isa. 40:31)

Satan's Lie: You are alone. You are weak. You do not matter. Judgment is yours.

> Day 1: The Account of Tamar
> Day 2: Act Two
> Day 3: From Lust to Hate
> Day 4: Desolation
> Day 5: Judgment

WEEK 4: JESUS, PETER, AND WATER SPORTS

God's Promise: God sees you for who you really are. You can do all things through Christ.

Satan's Lie: You are nothing. You can't turn from the past

> Day 1: It Is I
> Day 2: God of the House of God
> Day 3: What Does God Want from You?
> Day 4: God Sees You Exactly as Who He Made You to Be
> Day 5: Generational Sin

WEEK 5: BETRAYAL AND BOUNDARIES

God's Promise: God will never leave or stop loving you. Your voice is and should be heard. You can trust again. You don't have to be afraid.

Satan's Lie: No one loves you. You can't trust anyone. You don't matter. Everyone will leave you when they know who you really are.

> Day 1: But It Was YOU!
> Day 2: Can I Ever Trust Again?
> Day 3: Guarding Your "House" Part 1
> Day 4: Guarding Your "House" Part 2
> Day 5: God's Boundaries

WEEK 6: SATAN'S DEEDS / INVISIBLE TIES / RESULTING SIN

God's Promise: You will be separated from the abuser/s. The husband and wife shall become one.

Satan's Lie: You will always be tied to the abuser/s. Everyone is the same. Sex is only physical.

Day 1: What Is and What Should Never Be
Day 2: Signals and Stop Signs
Day 3: "Submission" Is Not Really a Four-Letter Word
Day 4: Sin Resulting from Abuse
Day 5: Un-forgiveness: The Tie That Binds

WEEK 7: TAKE BACK YOUR GARDENS

God's Promise: You are forgiven. You are clean, loved and beautiful. You can be free!

Satan's Lie: You'll never change. You're not forgiven. You are damaged goods.

Day 1: Who God Created You to Be. You, Specifically
Day 2: B. M. D. A. G. C. L. D. B. M. K. S. M. T. D. R. B. T. A. H. L. E. M. P. E.
Day 3: Temptations and Faith
Day 4: Gardens Are for Flowers, Not Weeds
Day 5: Emmanuel: God With Us

CPSIA information can be obtained
at www.ICGtesting.com
Printed in the USA
BVOW03s0440270717

489803BV00002BC/13/P